LEO ZANELLI
081 341 3655

Traditional Lake District Food

A TASTE OF
THE LAKE DISTRICT

Theodora FitzGibbon

Period photographs specially prepared by

George Morrison

Ward Lock Limited · London

for Mary Burkett
with affection and admiration

First published 1980 by Pan Books Ltd.
Cavaye Place, London SW10 9PG
and simultaneously in hardback by
Ward Lock Limited, 116 Baker Street, London W1M 2BB
A Pentos Company
© Theodora FitzGibbon 1980
ISBN 0 7063 6011 7
Filmset by
Northumberland Press Ltd,
Gateshead, Tyne and Wear
Printed in Great Britain by
Fletcher & Son Ltd, Norwich

ACKNOWLEDGEMENTS

We both want to thank the many people who gave us so much assistance during the research for this book: particularly Miss Mary Burkett, Director of Abbot Hall Gallery and Museum of Lakeland Life and Industry, Kendal, and her assistant Mr John Renton, for their immense help and patience; Mrs Jean Seymour of the Crag Cumbrian Restaurant, Bowness-on-Windermere, for giving me recipes and finding us unpublished photographs; Jean and Arthur Butterworth of White Moss House Hotel, Rydal Water, for their hospitality and recipes; Mrs Johnson and her daughter-in-law Barbara of Tullythwaite House, Underbarrow, for the fine food and the chance to taste the elusive char; also to Miss Simone Boddington of the Yan Tyan Tethera Restaurant, Keswick, for her help with traditional food; and last but certainly not least Mr John Tovey for giving us a most luxurious 'taste of the Lake District' at his superb hotel, Miller Howe.

Our thanks also to Mr Barber of the Lakeland Bookshop, Bowness, for getting us much needed books. A special mention to Mr Barry Crofts for letting us use some of his old photographs from his treasured albums, and also to Mrs Margaret Wilson of the Grasmere Gingerbread Shop for the photograph on page 77.

We also want to thank the Trustees of Dove Cottage for the photograph on page 6, and Mr Greenwood of the Cumberland Pencil Company for his kindness in letting us use the photograph on page 62. Photographs on pages 9, 10, 13, 14, 17, 21, 22, 26, 29, 30, 33, 34, 37, 38, 41, 42, 45, 46, 49, 53, 54, 57, 58, 61, 65, 66, 69, 70, 73, 74, 82, 86, 94, 98, 101, 102, 105, 106, 109, 110, 114, 118, 121, 122, 125 and 126 are reproduced by kind permission of Miss Burkett of Abbot Hall, Kendal; on pages 18, 50 and 117 by kind permission of Mr Elsby of Keswick Public Library; on pages 81, 85, 89, 90, 93 and 113 by kind permission of Mr Barry Croft, Bowness. The photograph on page 78 is by kind permission of Mrs Margaret Duff from her private collection, and the photograph on page 25 was kindly loaned by Mrs Veronica Rowe from her private collection.

Once again I must thank my local librarian Miss Paula O'Regan for her kindness in getting me out-of-print books, and also Miss Betty Searson of the Royal Dublin Society for her great help.

INTRODUCTION

The English Lake District is part of Cumbria, breathtaking in its beauty and varied scenery with its many mountains, fells, meres, tarns and lakes. Each one has its own charm and character encircled by hills which have an almost kaleidoscopic quality that changes the colour of the landscape from hour to hour. It was a Brythonic and Icelandic settlement enclosed by its hills, a race of hard-working people little influenced by the outside. Indeed, until early this century sheep were still counted in Celtic dialect, and many traces of Norse origin still remain.

Until the mid-18th century tourists as such did not go there and Thomas Gray the poet (1716–71) is credited with having been one of the first; it was his writings that stimulated public imagination and sent many visitors lakewards. Then, it was the time of the Romantic movement, sketchbooks and notebooks were *de rigeur*, and even small hand mirrors, for the 'thing to do' was to stand with your back to a view, manoeuvring the mirror until a special snapshot view was obtained. Many now-famous people came to live there and at the time some of them were very poor. Dorothy and William Wordsworth lived only on home-made bread, porridge, potatoes, milk and spring water, tea being too expensive, and they started growing vegetables in the garden of Dove Cottage, Grasmere. Others who lived there were Coleridge, Southey, De Quincey, Shelley, Ruskin, Matthew Arnold, Harriet Martineau, Mrs Radcliffe, Mrs Humphrey Ward; nearer to our own time, Beatrix Potter and Hugh Walpole all lived in that comparatively small area, as well as the philosopher Charles Lloyd, Bishop Watson and many more. Yet as De Quincey so rightly remarks, the notion of a 'Lake School' of poets was laughable – although they were friends their points of view were very different.

Such was the landscape that even a few miles of rough country meant that to visit your neighbour required either a horse, or a boat, or an arduous mountain trek. For instance, Coleridge's house – Greta Hall, Keswick, where Southey also lived – was in Cumberland, a good thirteen miles away from Grasmere in Westmorland where the Wordsworths lived, yet it is recorded that they often walked over to visit; Dorothy Wordsworth writes that she set out at dusk and arrived at Greta Hall around midnight.

This did not change all that much with the coming of the Kendal and Windermere Railway in 1847, for much of the countryside was not affected. However, it did bring many tourists to Windermere, at that time called Birthwaite, a hamlet with perhaps half a dozen houses. Bowness-on-Windermere was at that time quite a sizeable village, with a 15th-century church (built on the site of a 13th-century church), shops, two or three hotels, at least one of which was known in the early 18th century. By 1885 Windermere village had over forty lodging houses, the tourists flocked there and the prosperity they brought lightened the lot of many of the exceedingly poor inhabitants.

These tourists were enchanted with the comparatively new invention, the camera: the sketchbooks were left at home and the camera became the popular possession. Previously many artists and engravers had come to the Lake District, and now several photographers took their place. In 1854 there was A. Pettitt in Keswick with his Art Gallery and Portrait Studio; George Percy Abraham, an apprentice of his, who later set up his own shop in which two of his four sons joined him, George and Ashley, some of whose photographs appear in this book. Many others set up in Ambleside, Bowness and Kendal: such as George Waters, the Walmsley brothers, James Bankes, Lovell Mason, Mr Herbert and his sons and possibly others whose names are now forgotten. It is due to these men that we are able to piece together such a varied tapestry of 19th-century life in the Lake District.

The Lakeland people have a great integrity; they are charming, with a sense of fun yet a serious side. This serious side is shown in their interest in food, the standard being very high, from the inexpensive places to those in the upper bracket. This does not always obtain in parts of the world which cater for tourists! In general the food is of high quality, simply cooked and presented but full of good flavour. There are few regions of England which still have so many traditional foods for, even without much thought, Cumberland sausage, Cumberland ham, Cumberland sauce, and rum butter linger in one's mind, not forgetting the superb char for which this region is noted.

Let us enjoy, then, this 'Taste of the Lake District' remembering all the Lakelanders of the past, and also thinking of those of the present who uphold these splendid traditions.

Theodora FitzGibbon,
Atlanta,
Dalkey, Co Dublin,
Ireland.

January 1980

THE POET WORDSWORTH.

From a Daguerreotype formerly belonging to the
POET ROGERS, but now in possession of
Dr. CROMPTON, Manchester.

PHOTOGRAPHED BY R. CARLYLE, GRASMERE.
Copyright, registered.

ROBERT SOUTHEY'S GOOSEBERRY PIE

William Wordsworth is perhaps Cumbria's most famous son. He was born at Cockermouth to the north of the fell country, but went to the grammar school at Hawkshead (page 8). During his period at Cambridge University he came back for the holidays, spending some time with his sister, Dorothy, and Mary Hutchinson (whom he was later to marry) at Penrith. In 1799 William and Dorothy moved to Town End, Grasmere, now known as Dove Cottage and once an inn called the Dove and Olive-Bough. Although tiny it later housed the Wordsworths together with William's wife and three children, guests such as Coleridge, and other friends. William and Dorothy were great walkers and thought little of walking the thirteen miles from Grasmere over Dunmail Raise to visit Robert Southey and his family at Keswick (page 19). When they vacated the cottage and lived for a short while at the larger Allan Bank, it was taken by Thomas De Quincey who lived there with his wife and family for twenty-six years. Later the Wordsworths were to live at the larger Rydal Mount for thirty-seven years, where William died in April 1850. This house is lived in by his descendants and is open to the public, as is Dove Cottage.

'And now 'tis mine, perchance for life, dear Vale
Beloved Grasmere (let the wandering streams
Take up, the cloud-capt hills repeat, the name).
One of thy lowly dwellings is my home.'   William Wordsworth.

'I walked up to Mr Simpson's [father-in-law of De Quincey, at Nab Farm] to gather gooseberries ... I made tarts, pies etc. Wm stuck peas.'
7–10 June 1800, Journals of Dorothy Wordsworth.

ROBERT SOUTHEY'S GOOSEBERRY PIE

'Two gooseberry pies being supposed, their paste made at the same time, and indeed in one mass, the gooseberries gathered from the same bushes and of equal age, the sugar in just proportion, and clotted cream to eat with both, it follows that the largest is preferable. I love gooseberry pie ... and I think the case is plain.' It is quite possible that Dorothy Wordsworth could have got this recipe from Mrs Southey.

225 g (8 oz) pastry (see page 87)

For the filling

For a 1.1 litre (2 pint) pie dish	1 heaped tablespoon butter
700 g (1½ lb) green gooseberries	1 egg white and sugar for garnish
150 g (5 oz) sugar, or to taste	

First make the pastry, roll into a ball and leave in a cold place to rest. Top and tail the berries and mix with the sugar. Butter the dish, then put in the fruit. Dampen the edges and lay a strip of pastry around. Roll out the rest, brush the edge with egg white and lay it on. Brush the top with the remainder, sprinkle with sugar and bake at 200°C (400°F) or gas mark 6 for 30–40 minutes.

William Wordsworth, the poet (1770–1850) c. 1840s. From an old daguerreotype first belonging to the poet Samuel Rogers, rephotographed by R. Carlyle, Grasmere.

HAWKSHEAD BISCUITS

Flag Street, Hawkshead is so-called because of the flag stones placed over the stream, the water from which was drawn by the householders. The interlocking slate fence and the slate cladding on the walls are traditional to the area. Hawkshead, formerly a market town, is still very picturesque with its narrow streets and lanes, now usually thronged with tourists who come to see the old grammar school, founded by Archbishop Sandys in 1585. Wordsworth went to school there and carved his name, still to be seen, on his desk. There is also the cottage where he lodged with old Ann Tyson whom he revisited many times in later life. The church, St Michael's, dates from the 16th century, though there are records which show chapels belonging to Furness Abbey on the site at a much earlier date. There is an interesting altar tomb to William and Margaret Sandys dated 1578, in the northeast corner. In the fifth book of Wordsworth's The Prelude *he writes:*

'The self-same village church; I see her sit
(The throned Lady whom erewhile we hailed)
On her green hill.'

From the churchyard there is a charming view over Wordsworth's:

'... little town obscure,
A market village, seated in a tract
Of mountains, where my school-day time was pass'd.'

HAWKSHEAD BISCUITS

A traditional biscuit possibly enjoyed by the poet in his early life. Recipe from Mrs Elleray, c. 1895.

450 g (1 lb) plain flour
1 teaspoon baking powder
125 g (4 oz) butter
50 g (2 oz) castor sugar

1 large egg beaten with 300 ml (½ pint) milk
grated rind 1 lemon

Sift the flour and baking powder, then rub in the butter. Add the sugar and mix to a soft dough with the beaten egg and milk. Then mix in the grated lemon rind. Divide into about eight pieces; roll out on a floured surface to 1.5 cm (½ in) thick, prick all over with a fork and put on to a greased baking sheet. Bake at 180°C (350°F) or gas mark 4 for about 15–20 minutes.

HAWKSHEAD CAKE

This is a yeasted cake very similar to Christmas Bread (page 55) but soft brown sugar is used instead of white and the treacle is omitted.

Flag Street, Hawkshead, c. 1890. Photographed by Frith.

WESTMORLAND PEPPER CAKE

WESTMORLAND PEPPER CAKE

This traditional cake stems from the days in the 18th century when there was a flourishing trade with the West Indies and the Far East, where wool was exported for carpet making in exchange for spices, brown sugar, molasses and rum.

125 g (4 oz) butter
450 g (1 lb) plain flour
1 teaspoon baking powder
225 g (8 oz) sugar
125 g (4 oz) each: currants, raisins (Valencia if possible)
25 g (1 oz) chopped candied lemon peel

225 g (½ lb) black treacle, warmed
2 eggs
½ teaspoon ground cloves
1 teaspoon ground ginger
½ teaspoon ground black pepper

Sift the flour and baking powder, and rub in the butter into it. Add the sugar, dried fruit, spices and treacle mixed with the beaten eggs. Mix very well, and pour into a greased and lined 23 cm (9 in) cake tin and bake in a slow oven, 150°C (300°F) or gas mark 3, for about 2 hours. Cool on a wire rack and store for a few days in a tin before using.

OLD-FASHIONED PARKIN

125 g (4 oz) plain flour
½ teaspoon ground cinnamon
1 rounded teaspoon ground ginger
1 small teaspoon bicarbonate of soda
225 g (8 oz) medium oatmeal

50 g (2 oz) butter
25 g (1 oz) lard
225 g (8 oz) black treacle
225 g (8 oz) soft brown sugar
1 beaten egg
5–6 tablespoons milk

First line a square tin about 20 cm (8 in) with greased greaseproof paper. Then sieve together the flour, cinnamon, ginger and bicarbonate of soda; add oatmeal, mixing well. Heat together the butter, lard, treacle and sugar slowly, stirring well, and add it alternately to the flour mixture with the beaten egg. Finally add the milk and mix to form a fairly soft dough. Turn into the prepared tin and smooth the top over and bake at 150°C (300°F) or gas mark 3 for 50–60 minutes. Leave to cool, store in a tin and the next day cut into squares.

Mr and Mrs Handley of Garside, c. 1850. The costume detail in this very early photograph is interesting, the silk of Mrs Handley's dress being particularly fine.

HAVER or CLAP BREAD

Outside staircases were quite common early on, and some of these houses also had a small gallery at the top with struts like a staircase. This was known as a 'spinning gallery' although it was mainly used to store packed fleeces after sheep-shearing for it was both cool and damp.

The staple diet of many farm people in this part of the country was oatmeal. Wheat bread was sometimes baked, but in the main it was oat bread known as 'haver' bread, the word coming from the Old Norse word hafrar meaning oats. Often it was a broad, thin cake known as 'clap' bread from being clapped between the hands to make it thin, not unlike the present-day Norwegian flatbröd. It was baked on a circular iron griddle or bakestone, usually suspended over an open fire. Enough bread was baked in a single day to last for about a month, and it was stored in carved oak cupboards, often of great beauty. Celia Fiennes who travelled around England by horse in the 17th century wrote vividly about the making of clap bread near Kendal in 1698:

'... they mix their flour with water so soft as to rowle it in their hands into a ball, and then they have a board made round and something hollow in the middle rising by degrees all round to the edge a little higher, but so little as one would take it to be only a board warp'd, this is to cast out the cake thinn as a paper, and still they clap it and drive it round, and then they have a plaite of iron same size with their clap board and so shove off the cake on it, and so set it on the coales and bake it ...'

HAVER or CLAP BREAD

Today the method is simpler and oatcakes are very good to eat with butter, cheese, jam or honey, or especially with fish such as herrings.

225 g (8 oz) fine oatmeal
125 g (4 oz) wholewheat flour
1 teaspoon salt
25 g (1 oz) fresh yeast or 15 g ($\frac{1}{2}$ oz) dried

600 ml (1 pint) mixed tepid milk and water
oatmeal for rolling

Mix together the oatmeal, flour and salt. Dissolve the yeast in the tepid milk and water. Add to the oatmeal mixture, cover and leave to rise for an hour. Then mix well kneading with floured hands. Turn on to a surface sprinkled with oatmeal, and with the hands shape and flatten into cakes or squares. Have a greased griddle or heavy pan hot, and cook on one side until just firm and crisp. Lift out and either put them into a moderate oven, 180°C (350°F) or gas mark 4, cooked side down, or toast the uncooked side in front of the fire until crisp and pale brown. The flour makes them easier to handle, but originally they were made with all oatmeal.

See also Oat Biscuits (page 47), Oatmeal Bread (page 64), and Parkin (page 11).

An old stone farmhouse with an outside staircase, c. 1880.

BACON AND APPLE HOT POT

Glencoyne Farm was first built in 1629 by the Howard family, extended in the early 18th century. The photograph has many points of interest such as the fire-dog in front to stop the wood from falling out and the crane for roasting with an assortment of ratten-crooks. The big black pot at the side could be used for roasting, boiling or baking. In the wall on either side of the fireplace are two spice cupboards where the precious spices could be kept away from rodents and also warm and dry. The shepherd's crook is on the table, and on the wall is obviously a handsome belt probably won for wrestling: the two silver cups on the shelf are other trophies won for either raising champion sheep or at a country sport.

BACON AND APPLE HOT POT

1.4 kg (3 lb) boiling bacon	2 level tablespoons black treacle
450 g (1 lb) peeled, cored and	(molasses)
sliced apples	pepper
1 large sliced onion	1 medium cabbage heart,
a pinch of sage and thyme	quartered

Trim the bacon and cut into large cubes; soak these for at least 4 hours in cold water. Drain and put into a sauccpan with the apples, onion, herbs, treacle and pepper and cover with cold water. Bring to the boil and simmer gently for about 1 hour or until the bacon is quite tender. Add the cabbage, bring back to the boil, then simmer again until the cabbage is cooked. Taste for seasoning and serve with boiled potatoes, which can be added with the cabbage, but see that they are all the same size so that cooking is even. Serves about 6.

Variation: this was also put into a suet crust with a suet pastry lid (page 39) covered with a cloth or foil and steamed for about 3 hours.

In season, country housewives would also add some fresh damsons for which the Lyth Valley is famous. This gives a tart and unusual flavour to this good country dish. If bacon was scarce mutton was used.

Glencoyne Farm kitchen, Ullswater, c. 1880s.

BUTTERED SOPS

Many customs concerning births only died out in the first decade of this century in Westmorland and Cumberland. It was common for friends of the woman 'in the clouts' to be bidden to attend the birth when it was due, and these friends were ceremonially called. A big china dish of good quality was prepared full of rum butter (see page 59) and held in readiness for the event. This was given to the new mother first of all as it was thought to be a fine pick-me-up! At the same time the baby's head was washed with rum 'to make it stronger'. The old china rum butter dishes are now sought after as antiques.

Sometimes the midwives, locally called 'houdy-wives', cooked the food for the celebration feast. In 1818 William Fleming of Furness recorded in his diary: 'The Wife of a Farmer of mine was brought to Bed a few days ago and Preparations had been made previous to the expected event. As soon as the good Woman was delivered some Ale was put on the Fire with Spices to warm and a Cheese (better than Common) and a large loaf of fine Bread. The accoucheur [male midwives were common] cut a slice or two of the Cheese, then cross cut them into Pieces about the size of a Finger and Shook them in his Shirt lap: These were distributed among the unmarried Women to lay under their Pillows at Night to dream of. This cheese is called the Groaning Cheese of which all present ate heartily and drank the warm Ale mixed with Rum or Brandy after which the married Women leapt over a Besom or Birch Broom and she who did not clear the Broom was pronounced the next for the Straw.'

All relatives were invited to the christening as well as many friends and the traditional dish was called 'buttered sops'. Presents to the baby consisted of silver coins and another custom which still occurs occasionally is to give an egg and a pinch of salt to the newborn. Salt was considered a charm against bad luck and fairies.

BUTTERED SOPS

Joseph Budworth recorded this recipe in his diary in 1792.

'Upon the day of celebrating the ceremony, all the matrons in the neighbourhood assemble at the joyful house, and each brings as a present to the good woman in the straw either one pound of sugar, one pound of butter, or sixpennyworth of wheaten bread. The bread is cut in thin slices and placed in rows one above the other in a large kettle of 20 or 30 gallons. The butter and sugar are dissolved in a separate one, and then poured upon the bread, where it continues until it has boiled for some space and the bread is perfectly saturated with the mixture. It is served ... by way of a dessert.'

Young mother in a Westmorland cottage, c. 1890. Photographed by George Abraham.

DERWENTWATER DUCKLING

Greta Hall was the home of the poet Samuel Taylor Coleridge from 1800. He rented it for a nominal rent from William Jackson, who had made a fortune from his carrier business and was anxious to encourage the arts and to live the life of a gentleman. To begin with he lived in half the house, but later another poet, Robert Southey, and his family also moved in and he gave up his quarters. Coleridge wrote to Southey in May 1803: 'This house is full twice as large as we want; it hath more rooms in it than Alfoxden; you might have a bedroom, parlour, etc. etc. . . . I know no place in which you and Edith would find yourself so well suited.' At the end of August that same year Southey and his family arrived and were to stay there for forty years. When Coleridge found the responsibilities of marriage too much and moved off, Southey looked after his family as his own; when Coleridge returned from Malta in 1804 he stayed more with the Wordsworths at Grasmere than at Greta Hall.

Many famous literary figures stayed there: Samuel Rogers, Charles Lamb and his sister Mary, Hazlitt, Sir Walter Scott are to mention a few; and Wordsworth and his sister Dorothy often walked from Grasmere not only by the road but also along the moorland track which strikes from Thirlmere to Watendlath, and so by Ashness Bridge on to the Borrowdale Road, nearly a couple of miles from Greta Hall.

It was at Greta Hall that Southey was offered and accepted his Poet Laureateship. 'Coleridge had got a blazing fire in his study; which is a large antique, ill-shaped room, with an old-fashioned organ, never played upon, big enough for a church, shelves of scattered folios, an Aeolian harp, and an old sofa, half bed, etc. And all looking out upon the last fading view of Skiddaw, a nearby mountain, and his broad-breasted brethren: what a night! Here we stayed three full weeks, in which time I visited Wordsworth's cottage, where we stayed a day or two with the Clarksons [the anti-slavery crusader] good people, and most hospitable.'

Charles Lamb, 1775–1834.

Greta Hall, Keswick, c. 1880.

DERWENTWATER DUCKLING

By kind permission of Jean Seymour, from *Lakeland Cookery*.

A 1.8 kg (4 lb) duckling	2 tablespoons brandy or rum
salt and pepper	2 teaspoons cornflour
4 small onions stuck with 1 clove each	150 ml ($\frac{1}{4}$ pint) giblet stock
a little oil or butter	4 tablespoons Cumberland Sauce (page 80)

Wipe the bird and sprinkle inside and out with salt and pepper; put the onions stuck with cloves inside the body. Rub with oil and roast at 200°C (400°F) or gas mark 6 for 1 hour 40 minutes, basting from time to time.

When cooked, pour off excess fat. Warm the brandy, pour it over and set alight. Put duck on to a warmed serving dish, stir the cornflour into the pan juices, add the stock, and then add the Cumberland Sauce. Stir and simmer for about 5 minutes. Pour a little sauce over the duck and serve the rest in a sauce-boat. Serves 4.

ROWANBERRY JELLY

Beatrix Potter (1866–1943) lived for many years in the Lake District at Hill Top in the village of Near Sawrey between Windermere and Esthwaite Water. She moved there in 1906 and it is there that she wrote most of her world famous children's stories. She married Mr Heelis and invested the income from her books in the breeding of pedigree Herdwick sheep, becoming for many years the chairman of the Herdwick Sheep Breeders Association. On her death she bequeathed her house and farms to the National Trust and at Hill Top you will see some of her original manuscripts and a small notebook with watercolour sketches and notes of various sheep markings. Wray Castle is a large 19th-century Gothic building, overlooking Windermere, which Beatrix Potter's father often rented for family summer holidays. It is now a boarding school for Merchant Navy radio-officer cadets.

Up until about the 1930s preserves and wines were always done by the lady of the house in the stillroom which was part of her demesne.

ROWANBERRY JELLY

The rowan or mountain ash was sacred to the gods of the ancient Gaels and the Scandinavians, who ate the berries believing they had power over evil spirits; a branch was hung in Cumbrian stables and stalls to protect the animals from harm. A rowan stick was used to stir the cream before butter-making and sometimes garlands of rowan leaves were wrapped around the churn or even a stick was put into the churn to ensure that the butter would 'take'.

Put about 1.4 kg (3 lb) of rowan berries and 2 large chopped unpeeled or cored apples into a large saucepan and barely cover with water. Bring to the boil and simmer for about 40 minutes. Drain through muslin or a jelly-bag overnight, but do not squeeze the fruit. The next day add 450 g (1 lb) sugar to every pint (600 ml) of juice, stir until the sugar is dissolved, then boil rapidly for about 15–20 minutes until setting point is reached. Pour into hot, sterilized jars, cover, label and store. It is delicious with lamb or game.

This recipe can also be used for redcurrant jelly, damson jelly, blackberry or elderberry jelly; the apples can be omitted in these four and the juice of a large lemon added. Elderberries are used a lot in the Lake District, and elderberry wine is often used in meat casseroles, and sometimes in Cumberland Sauce.

DAMSON WINE

The damsons from the Lyth valley southwest of Kendal are exceptionally fine. This recipe is also for elderberries or blackberries. Stalk and wash 1.8 kg (4 lb) sound, ripe fruit. Pour over 4.5 litres (1 gallon) boiling water and when cool, mash the fruit well. Add 1 teaspoon Pektolase and a Campden tablet, cover and leave for 3 days. Then strain and press. Add 1.4 kg (3 lb) sugar, port yeast and yeast nutrient, then another 225 g (½ lb) sugar dissolved in a little of the liquor. Keep covered for 1 week and put into a fermenting bottle with an airlock. Do not bottle until it is clear and all fermentation has stopped. Mature for at least 9 months.

Beatrix Potter (second from left) her brother Bertram, Mrs Potter and a friend at Wray Castle, 1881. Photograph taken by her brother Rupert Potter.

EASTER-LEDGE PUDDING

The Jolly Boys were associated with the pace-egg mummers' play, pace-egg being derived from 'paschal', and this took place at Eastertide, usually on Good Friday. The play had a curious plot and characters included Lord Nelson, the Doctor, Bessy Brown Bags and Tosspot, and basically it was a morality play with right triumphing over evil. The Jolly Boys called at houses with their play and asked for pennies and pace-eggs. Traditional fare is recorded by William Fleming in the 19th century: 'It has been an Immemorial Custom in this corner of England, on Good Friday to eat ... Fig Sewe, made of Figs cut in quarters, with Wheaten Bread cut into small Square Pieces and boiled in Ale or Beer seasoned with Sugar or Treacle and nutmeg ... this is much relished ... and eaten to Dinner before salt or Fresh Fish.' Pace-eggs were hard-boiled eggs dyed with onion skins, oranges or daffodils, cochineal etc. Groves Brothers, the dyers at Kendal, used to leave out vats of dye from which the children filled jam jars. On Easter Monday in Kendal they would go up to Kendal Castle Hill and roll these eggs, the winner being the one whose eggs stayed unbroken. Adults played Grandy Needles, a game played by making an archway of hands, then running through singing the song 'Grandy Needles, Grandy Needles, set, bump, set ...' and making three 'bumps'.

Easter-ledge pudding was also traditional to Easter. The name is thought to be derived through 'Easter-logia' from 'Astrologia' which is given in 1548 as an alternative name for bistort (Polygonum bistorta), a pretty plant with pale pink 'bottle-brush' flowers, from which the pudding is made. In 'The Folklore of the Lake District' by Marjorie Rowling the following traditional family recipe from the 1870s is given.

EASTER-LEDGE PUDDING

From Mrs Scott of Wigton, Cumberland from her great-great grandmother.

450 g (1 lb) approx young bistorts and young nettle tops	125 g (4 oz) pot barley
	½ teaspoon salt
1 large onion	

Chop the greens and onion finely and sprinkle the washed barley among them, adding the salt. Boil in a muslin bag for about 2 hours. Before serving, beat the mixture in a dish with 1 egg, a large knob of butter, salt and pepper. Some people add a cup of oatmeal. Make into a cake and fry in fat. Eat with bacon and eggs, or fried potatoes. Chopped hard-boiled egg can also be added and in some parts of Cumberland, dandelion or Lady's Mantle (Alchemilla vulgaris) is added as well. It is obviously a very good spring tonic and good with its accompaniments.

CUMBERLAND TOFFEE

450 g (1 lb) soft brown sugar	125 g (4 oz) butter
125 g (4 oz) black treacle or golden syrup	1 tablespoon milk
	1 tablespoon vinegar
1 tablespoon water	

Bring all ingredients except the vinegar, slowly to the boil, stirring all the time until it reaches 140°C (275°F). This should take about 20 minutes. Stir in the vinegar and pour into a well-greased shallow tin. As it is setting, score into small squares. It can also be used as a dip for making toffee apples.

The Jolly Boys at Hill Top Farm, home of Beatrix Potter. Photographed by Beatrix Potter, 1908.

CHICKEN AND HAM MOULD

Matthew Arnold was the son of the famous Dr Thomas Arnold, head-master of Rugby School. He lived for many years at Foxe Howe near Rydal, one of the most beautiful parts of the Lake District.

During a long period of ill-health Harriet Martineau, the writer and pro-Abolitionist, lived at 'The Knoll' Ambleside. In the winter she enjoyed sitting in her room watching the lights come on across the valley in her neighbours' houses, and remarked that Foxe Howe was always the first to light up.

'Max with shining yellow coat,
Silken ears and dewlap throat.'   *Matthew Arnold.*

CHICKEN AND HAM MOULD

1 boiling chicken about 1.8 kg (4 lb)	450 g (1 lb) raw lean ham or bacon
½ lemon	25 g (1 oz) gelatine
1 small blade mace	1 tablespoon finely chopped parsley
1 medium onion	2 hard-boiled eggs
salt and pepper	1 small bunch watercress

Wash and dry the chicken, then rub all over inside and out with the cut lemon. Put it into a large saucepan with the lemon, cover with boiling water, bring back to the boil, then skim. Add the mace and onion, salt and pepper. Bring back to the boil, then reduce to a simmer, cover and cook for about 1½ hours. Test at 1 hour to see if it is getting tender. Half an hour before the chicken is ready, add the ham cut into cubes and trimmed of any fat or bone. When cooked leave to cool in the stock, then lift out the chicken on to a dish, skin and take off all the meat and put on to a separate plate or dish. Lift out the ham cubes, then put back the carcase, and boil again until the liquid is reduced by one-third. Let the stock get cold and remove any fat from the top. Arrange the chicken and ham which has been chopped into neat pieces in a wetted mould or deep dish with the sliced hard-boiled eggs and sprinkle with the chopped parsley. Heat up about 725 ml (1¼ pints) of the chicken stock and dissolve the gelatine in it. Taste for seasoning. Strain over the meat, cover with foil or a plate and leave for a few hours to set in the refrigerator. To turn out, wrap a hot cloth around and put a dish on top, then turn quickly. Garnish with fresh watercress. Serves at least 8 cut into slices.

It is very good served with jacket baked potatoes and salad.

Matthew Arnold, 1822–1888, poet and literary critic, with his dog Max at Foxe Howe, near Rydal, 27 June 1883. Photographed by Bertram Buxton of Foxwarren.

LAKELAND FINGERS

The fine Victorian interior opposite is a good example of the furnishings of that period, and it is interesting to note that electric light has been installed. The Cumbrian people are fond of cakes and many traditional kinds are still made and eaten there. Spices and ginger figure in many of them, stemming from the days of trade with the West Indies and the Far East.
See also: Grasmere Gingerbread, page 76.

LAKELAND FINGERS

This recipe occurs in an early edition of *Mrs Beeton*.

450 g (1 lb) plain flour	2 level teaspoons cream of tartar
pinch of salt	225 g (8 oz) soft brown sugar
3–4 level teaspoons ground ginger	225 g (8 oz) butter or margarine
1 level teaspoon bicarbonate of soda	

Sift all dry ingredients into a mixing bowl, then rub in the butter until it resembles fine breadcrumbs. Put into a square or oblong shallow tin and press down lightly to a layer about 2 cm ($\frac{3}{4}$ in) thick. Bake at 180°C (350°F) or gas mark 4 for 20–30 minutes. Cut into about 24 fingers while it is still warm.

WESTMORLAND DREAM CAKE

Recipe from Mary Chadwick, aunt of Simone Boddington who owns and runs the good Yan Tyan Tethera restaurant in Keswick.

Before the Lakeland tea-party, c. 1900.

125 g (4 oz) butter
125 g (4 oz) plain flour
25 g (1 oz) soft brown sugar

Rub the fat into the sifted flour and add the brown sugar. Put into a Swiss Roll tin, flatten out and bake for 20 minutes at 180°C (350°F) or gas mark 4. Cool in tin.

225 g (8 oz) soft brown sugar	125 g (4 oz) chopped walnuts
25 g (1 oz) plain flour	75 g (3 oz) grated coconut
pinch of salt	$\frac{1}{2}$ level teaspoon baking powder

Mix these ingredients together, then add:

2 beaten eggs

Mix well, spread on top of the cooked cake and bake for a further 20 minutes with the oven at the same temperature. Serves 6.

MEG'S SHORTBREAD

Blend together 125 g (4 oz) sifted icing sugar and 350 g (12 oz) sifted self-raising flour. Rub in 225 g (8 oz) unsalted butter to make a dough. Do not add any liquid. Roll out to 1.5 cm ($\frac{1}{2}$ in), cut into rounds and prick the tops lightly with a fork. Put on to a greased baking sheet and bake for about 20 minutes, or until a pale golden brown in a moderate oven, 180°C (350°F) or gas mark 4. Makes 16–20 small shortbread biscuits.

CUMBRIAN LEMON CAKE

Shelley was another poet who lived for a while near Keswick; owing to a difference of opinion with Southey who had settled at Greta Hall, see page 19, his stay was not a long one. In February 1812 Shelley left Keswick for Ireland and never came back.

'These gigantic mountains piled on each other, these waterfalls, these million shaped clouds, tinted by the varying colours of innumerable rainbows hanging between yourself and a lake as smooth and dark as a plain of polished jet – oh, these are sights attunable to the contemplation.

'Snow vapours, tinted by the loveliest colours of refraction, pass far below the summits of these giant rocks. The scene, even in a winter's sunset, is inexpressibly lovely. What will it be in summer?' Percy Bysshe Shelley at Keswick, 1811.

However, Coleridge thought that winter was the best period to see the Lake District, for he wrote: 'Summer is not the season for this country ... then it is like a theatre at noon.'

CUMBRIAN LEMON CAKE

125 g (4 oz) butter	juice and grated rind 1 lemon
50 g (2 oz) lard	50 g (2 oz) chopped candied
150 g (5 oz) castor sugar	lemon peel
2 large eggs	1 tablespoon milk
225 g (8 oz) self-raising flour, sifted	

Cream the butter, lard and sugar until well blended. Then add the eggs singly with about a tablespoon of flour with each. Fold in the rest of the flour, then add the lemon juice, finely grated rind and chopped candied lemon peel. Mix well and add the milk only if the mixture seems too stiff, as it should be of firm dropping consistency. Lightly grease an 18 cm (7 in) tin with a removable base, pour in the mixture and bake at 180°C (350°F) or gas mark 4 for about 1½ hours. Let it cool for 5 minutes before removing from the tin and cooling on a rack. It can be served with lemon curd or cut across sandwich-fashion and spread with it, but it is extremely good as it is.

GINGER APPLES

Make a syrup with 900 g (2 lb) sugar and 850 ml (1½ pints) water by boiling it for 15 minutes. Then peel, core and cut 900 g (2 lb) apples into quarters (keep in lightly salted water to prevent discolouration). Add 125 g (4 oz) shredded crystallized ginger to the syrup, then put in the apples and boil gently for about 15–20 minutes or until the apples are opaque. Put into jars, seal down and store as for jam.

These ginger apples are delicious with ice-cream or as a sauce with cold pork or bacon. Makes about 2.3 kg (5 lb).

Chester Hill, near Keswick, the house where Shelley lived.

COUNTRY POT-ROASTED CHICKEN

Although not born in the Lake District, John Ruskin, 1819–1900, was a devotee from his first visit at the age of twelve when he rhymed in his journal: 'Our apartment was shown – to the window we flew – But, oh, what a prospect awaited our view!' Later he was to write: 'I went out, and in the heart of Langdale Pikes found the loveliest rock-scenery, chased with silver waterfalls, that I ever set foot or heart upon.' In 1871 he bought Brantwood and ten acres of land on the eastern shore of Coniston which had 'the finest view I know in Cumberland or Lancashire, with the sunset visible over the same'. He left Brantwood for periods but as his health deteriorated he was to stay there until his death, looked after by his cousin Mrs Severn and her family, see page 55. He was buried in Coniston churchyard among the fells he loved. Brantwood is now open to the public during the summer months.

Coniston Water is the third longest of the lakes being about 8 kilometres (5 miles) from Waterhead to Nibthwaite; it is 500 m ($\frac{1}{3}$ mile) wide, except approaching the outlet, and the greatest depth is 55 m (183 ft)' The angling there is good with a variety of fish.

COUNTRY POT-ROASTED CHICKEN

1.8 kg (4 lb) chicken and giblets	4 medium onions, sliced
salt and pepper	4 medium leeks, sliced
2 tablespoons chicken fat or oil	900 g (2 lb) potatoes
125 g (4 oz) lean bacon, chopped	a little seasoned flour

For the stuffing

Liver of the bird	breadcrumbs
125 g (4 oz) sausagemeat	pinch of thyme
1 heaped tablespoon fresh	1 tablespoon chopped parsley

Take the giblets from the bird, remove the liver, then cover the giblets well with cold water. Season with a little salt and pepper and boil for about 30–40 minutes. Strain and cool. Wipe the bird inside and out and sprinkle with salt. Chop the chicken liver finely and mix it with the other stuffing ingredients. Take out any lumps of fat from the bird and fill with the stuffing mixture, either crop or body end. Secure with a small skewer. Heat up the dripping or oil, fry the bacon and lightly brown the bird all over. Put it into an ovenproof dish with the onions and leeks, green part as well, and season. Pour over the giblet stock, warmed, bring to the boil, then cover and cook in a moderate oven 180°C (350°F) or gas mark 4 for about 1$\frac{1}{2}$ hours.

Meanwhile peel the potatoes and cut them into regular, thick slices. Blanch them in boiling water for about 5 minutes then drain. Toss them lightly in seasoned flour, then add them to the casserole, adding a little more liquid if needed but do not swamp it. Cover and continue cooking for a further 25–30 minutes or until the potatoes are ready. Serves 4–6.

John Ruskin and Mrs Severn on Coniston Water, c. 1890s.

CUMBERLAND SAUSAGE

Grisedale is a pretty village south of Patterdale. The name means 'the dale of wild pigs' which no doubt at one time roamed the nearby forest.

CUMBERLAND SAUSAGE

This is a fine traditional sausage which can be found all over the Lake District. One wonders if such a sausage was first made from the flesh of the wild pigs!

It is made solely from fresh pork and herbs, each butcher having his own recipe, and fine ones are to be found in Keswick, Penrith, Kendal and Bowness to mention a few. Unlike the usual sausage it is not formed into links but made in one continuous strip sometimes several feet long, from which the amount required is cut off. Because the ends are open it is best to bake it in a moderate oven, 180°C (350°F) or gas mark 4, for about 30–40 minutes. It should be pricked with a fork at regular intervals and turned once during cooking. Some cooks do grill this sausage but as it has a high meat content which should be cooked through it is best to use the oven.

Traditional recipes give the following amounts of pork to be used: 4 parts of lean pork to 2 parts belly of pork and 1 part back fat, well seasoned, minced and flavoured with a little sage, rosemary and thyme to taste. Cumberland Sausage seasoning is given as: 24% ground white pepper, 1% ground cayenne pepper, 1% ground nutmeg, 74% fine salt. 12 g ($\frac{1}{2}$ oz) of this mixture should be added to each 450 g (1 lb) meat.

The adventurous will find them well worth making and your butcher should be able to advise you on finding where to get the skins.

In these parts they are served with potatoes and apple sauce.

CUMBERLAND APPLE SAUCE

450 g (1 lb) cooking apples
50–75 g (2–3 oz) brown sugar according to taste
pinch of ground nutmeg or mace
squeeze of lemon

Peel, core and slice the apples and cook in about 4–6 tablespoons water and half the sugar until they are soft and fluffy. Add the rest of the sugar to taste, the spice, and beat well. Then add the squeeze of lemon and mix well. Serve warm. It also goes well with roast pork, duck and goose, see page 75. It is good cold with cold birds or meat.

The post-cart at Grisedale Bridge, c. 1900.

TATIE-POT

Life was hard for the Lakeland shepherd and also for his dogs, a short-haired breed that evolved over the centuries and are known as 'cur' dogs. Herdwick sheep are known for their ability to stay on their 'heaf' and not to stray but there are times when they wander over the watershed into an adjoining valley and get lost. However, the lamb in the photograph looks more like a Swaledale or Fell sheep. For hundreds of years Cumbrian shepherds have held 'Shepherds' Meets' at certain times of the year to return to their owners stray sheep that have been found on the fells. This was also the occasion for a 'Merry Neet' (night) when there was horse-racing, hound trailing, wrestling, fiddling, singing, and often hunting the next day. Certain classical places were known for these 'merry neets': the summit of the High Street range; the Old Dun Bull at Mardale and the Kirkstone House Inn, see page 52. The traditional food was tatie-pot, huge pies and beer.

Shepherd-farmers in Cumberland and Westmorland are known for their independence, learning and good manners. Coleridge in Biographia Literaria remarked on the high calibre of their thoughts, feelings, language and manners and attributed it to much reading of the Bible and liturgy.

TATIE-POT

This is the most succulent and delicious hot-pot, always served with pickled red cabbage.

700 g (1½ lb) potatoes	salt and freshly ground black
2 large onions	pepper

Shepherd with his sheepdogs and the strayed lamb, c. 1890.

900 g (2 lb) middle neck of lamb	450 ml (¾ pint) approx stock or water
350 g (12 oz) black pudding	1 tablespoon dripping or butter red cabbage, see below

Peel and slice the potatoes fairly thickly, then peel and slice the onions and trim the meat of fat, gristle and bone and cut into convenient pieces. Skin and slice the black pudding. Using a deep casserole or ovenproof dish, layer potatoes, onions, meat and black pudding in that order, seasoning well and ending with a thick layer of potatoes. Heat the stock and pour over to barely cover, put the lid on, slightly greased, and cook at 170°C (325°F) or gas mark 3 for about 2 hours. Take off the lid, brush the potatoes with the melted fat and sprinkle with salt, then return to the oven set at 180°C (350°F) gas mark 4 for a further 40 minutes or until the top is browned nicely. It can cook for longer time if the oven is set a little lower without coming to any harm. Serves at least 4 hungry people.

RED CABBAGE PICKLED

Shred finely a medium sized red cabbage, sprinkle with salt, cover and leave to stand overnight. The next day drain off the salt and pack into wide-necked jars. Boil together 600 ml (1 pint) malt vinegar with 1 tablespoon sugar and 1 tablespoon pickling spice, for about 10 minutes, cool slightly and pour over the cabbage covering it well. Tie down and leave for at least a week but it will keep indefinitely. A few slices of raw beetroot added give a fine deep red colour. Traditionally served cold, although you may prefer it heated up.

MUTTON OR LAMB HOTPOT

All methods are used to see that the flock gets fodder in the wintertime, see also pages 35 and 38. There is an interesting dialect way of counting sheep in Cumbria which is similar to that which was used in Wales, Cornwall and Brittany and has lasted since Celtic times when Cumbria was part of the great Celtic kingdom of Strathclyde. There are still shepherds who can recite these numerals although the tradition is rapidly dying out. It appears that the sheep were counted as follows: yan, taen, tedderte, medderte, pimp, haata, slaata, lowra, dowra, dick. This is the Coniston dialect from one to ten. The spelling varies a little from place to place.

'Sing, my bonny harmless sheep
That feed upon the mountain steep;
Bleating sweetly as ye go
Through the winter's frost and snow'   Old Cumbrian spinning song.

MUTTON OR LAMB HOTPOT

4 thick, lean mutton chops
a little oil, about 2 tablespoons
4 medium onions
6 medium carrots
6 medium potatoes
sprinkling of flour

$\frac{1}{4}$ teaspoon dried marjoram or
  thyme
1 level tablespoon brown sugar
1 pint good stock
salt and black pepper

Trim the chops and take out any bone, then season them well. Heat the oil and brown them on both sides. Prepare the vegetables and slice them up, seeing that the potatoes are fairly thickly sliced. Soften the carrots and onions in the oil the meat was cooked in, and add them to the meat, with the sprinkling of flour, the herbs and brown sugar. Mix well and barely cover with the hot stock. Season with salt and pepper. Arrange the potatoes thickly over the top and rub them over with any fat left in the pan, otherwise use a little butter. Cover well and cook in the oven at 170°C (325°F) or gas mark 3 for about 2 hours. Half an hour before they are cooked take off the lid to let the potatoes get brown. Serves 4.

Feeding the Herdwick sheep from a back-pack, c. 1890.

MUTTON AND LEEK PUDDING

The dark coloured sheep on the left of the photograph are Herdwicks, believed to have been introduced to this district by the Norsemen. They are extremely hardy and can withstand bad weather conditions. Another advantage is that they do not wander but stay on their own 'heaf'. The sheep on the other side are Swaledale and sometimes they are crossed with the Herdwick, consequently the purebred Herdwick is becoming increasingly rare. Herdwick wool fetches less than Swaledale, but the Herdwick has a denser coat. The sheep are gathered together and brought down from the fells for dipping and feeding before lambing: also in July for clipping (see page 40) and later for dipping. In the autumn they are once again brought down before being sent to their winter grazing grounds.

Beatrix Potter, the famous writer of children's stories (see page 21) invested the income from her books in Lakeland sheep farms and was for many years chairman of the Herdwick Sheep Breeders Association. Herdwick sheep vary in colour from dark grey to a beautiful mahogany brown and are very picturesque. See also page 37.

MUTTON AND LEEK PUDDING

This is a most warming and delicious winter dish.

900 g (2 lb) mutton without bone and not too much fat	*For the suet crust*
3 sheep's kidneys	225 g (8 oz) flour
1 onion	125 g (4 oz) grated suet or margarine
3 medium leeks	pinch of salt

1 sprig of chopped thyme and 1 of parsley
salt and pepper
300 ml ($\frac{1}{2}$ pint) approx mutton stock

approx 3–4 tablespoons water

Mix the suet with the flour and salt, then add enough water to make a soft, but firm dough. Roll into a ball and leave in a cool place while preparing the meat.

Take any bone, gristle or fat from the meat. Skin the kidney and remove the core then cut them and the lamb into small cubes. Roll them in seasoned flour. Prepare the vegetables and use some of the green part of the leeks as well as the white. Chop the onion and leeks into chunks.

Roll out the pastry, and cut off enough for the lid. Then take a 1.4 litres ($2\frac{1}{2}$ pints) pudding basin and grease and line it with about two-thirds of the pastry. Fill up the basin to about 2.5 cm (1 in) from the top with the meat and vegetables, also the herbs. Pack down well, add the stock, and the pastry lid, then cover with foil and tie down securely. Boil, or steam over boiling water, for about 3 hours. In winter, country women might also add some rowan berries or pickled damsons to the pudding. Serves about 4.

Shepherd on horseback driving his sheep down to the valley, c. 1900.

CLIPPING-TIME PUDDING

'*Two things ought to be seen in the lake country: sheep-washing and sheep-shearing ... (the sheep) are flung on their backs into the lap of a clipper seated on a long kind of settle – "sheep forms" they are called – who tranquilly tucks the little pointed head under his arm, and clips away at the under part of the wool, taking care to keep the fleece unbroken; the art being to hold the middle way, and neither to graze the skin by going too close, nor to loosen the fleece by cutting above the welted fibres. All four feet are now tied together, and the beast is hauled round as a solid kind of rug, when its back is sheared in the same way, the fleece hanging down like a bit of carpet or a small crib blanket. The little figures of the boys learning of the men ... the pretty young house-girls, looking so quiet and gentle, dressed in their Sunday best and carrying great jugs of beer – the strongest that can be brewed – laughing and yet shy, as they penetrate the mass of men and animals in the yard ... and the hot summer sun shining over all. For the first fortnight in July you may take your choice of the farms all over the country, small or large according to your liking; wanting no other guidance than the incessant bleating you will hear from daybreak to sunset, with the loud barking of the sheep dogs and the rough voices of the men directing.*'

E. Lynn Linton, 1822–98.

The fell farmer's method of clipping was from the back up to the neck, while the low farmer clipped all round. After clipping, the sheep is marked with tar from the 'ruddlepot' before going back to the fell. The whole procedure is enlivened with a 'boon' meal of bread and cheese with plenty of ale in the evenings.

'*There's no' but a fortni't between a good clip and a bad 'un.*'   Old saying.

CLIPPING-TIME PUDDING

This is a traditional pudding now seldom seen in these days of the machine.

125 g (4 oz) rice	125 g (4 oz) currants
600 ml (1 pint) milk	125 g (4 oz) raisins
75 g (3 oz) sugar	1 tablespoon butter or the
1 level teaspoon ground	marrow from 2 cooked beef
cinnamon	marrow bones
1 large egg, beaten	a pinch of salt

First blanch the rice in a little boiling, salted water, then strain and cook it slowly in the milk. Add the sugar and cinnamon, mix well and bring to the boil, then cook gently until the rice begins to soften. Add the beaten egg, the fruit and stir well, then add the butter or beef marrow cut into small pieces and season. Put into an ovenproof dish and bake at 200°C (400°F) or gas mark 6 for about 20 minutes. Serves 4.

Sheep-shearing time, 1870.

BEEFSTEAK PIE WITH CHEESE CRUST

The famous Grasmere Sports, an important date in the Lake District's sporting events, take place on the nearest Thursday to 20 August, and are attended by as many as 10,000 people. They are thought to have grown out of wrestling contests formerly held next to the Red Lion after the rush bearing procession (page 76) but by 1852 were established east of the village, with other events such as the fantastic guides' race, a fell race up and down Butter Crags near Greenhead Ghyll, a very steep fellside, and hound trailing (page 48). There is also pole vaulting, sprinting and of course Cumberland and Westmorland wrestling. Quantities of Grasmere gingerbread (page 76) are consumed with other good Cumbrian fare. Christopher North (Professor Wilson), editor of Blackwood's Magazine, gives us this description of a Lakeland breakfast, c. 1810:

'*Mrs Bell of the Red Lion Grassmere (sic) can give a breakfast with any woman in England. She bakes incomparable bread ... what butter! Before it a primrose must hide its unyellowed head. Then jam of the finest quality, gorse, raspberry and strawberry ... Hens cackle that the eggs are fresh and those shrimps were scraping the sands last night in Whitehaven sea. What glorious bannocks of barley meal, crisp wheaten cakes too! Do not our good sir, appropriate that cut of pickled salmon ... One might live a thousand years and yet never weary of such mutton ham ... virgin honey, cold pigeon pie, beefsteak with potatoes.*'

BEEFSTEAK PIE WITH CHEESE CRUST

There was not a lot of beef eaten in Cumbria, mutton and pork or

Grasmere Sports, 1897.

bacon being the chief meats, but the cheaper cuts were well utilized to make good, filling meals.

900 g (2 lb) stewing steak	pinch mixed herbs
a little flour	pinch of ground nutmeg, salt
2 tablespoons dripping or oil	and pepper
2 medium onions, finely chopped	2 whole cloves
4 medium carrots, thinly sliced	600 ml (1 pint) beef stock

For the crust
125 g (4 oz) plain flour
50 g (2 oz) margarine or butter
75 g (3 oz) grated Lancashire or
   Cheddar cheese

Trim the meat of fat and gristle and cut it into small cubes; roll in seasoned flour. Heat the fat or oil and soften the onions in it, also the carrots. Put them into a fireproof dish and add the meat to the fat and brown quickly all over. Add the rest of the ingredients, pouring over the stock last and adding a little more if needed. It should just cover the meat. Bring to the boil, cover and cook in a slow to moderate oven, 170°C–180°C (325°F–350°F) or gas marks 3–4 for about 1½ hours. Meanwhile make the crust by sifting the flour with a little salt, and then rubbing in the margarine well. Finally add the cheese and mix thoroughly. Sprinkle this over the top of the casserole and bake at 180°C (350°F) or gas mark 4 for about 30 minutes or until it is golden brown. Serves 4–6.

BRAWN

Wrestling is a traditional Cumbrian sport and unlike wrestling anywhere else. Its origins are obscure, some think it to have been introduced by the Norse–Irish colonists in the 10th century, but there is no firm evidence. However it is deeply entrenched in Lakeland traditions with its heroes and champions who ranged from George Steadman of Asby, near Appleby (who between 1865 and 1900 when he was 54 had won the Heavyweight Championship at Grasmere Sports seventeen times), to Christopher North (Professor Wilson), editor of Blackwood's Magazine, *a great wrestling man who wrote the following about it in the magazine in 1823:*

'Each man faces his opponent and proceeds to "tak' hod". Each wrestler must lock his hands by the fingers behind his opponent's back before either can attempt to throw the other. This takes time and a period of heaving and straining goes on. Nothing appears to be happening, then suddenly one wrestler heaves his opponent off his feet, holds him up and then hurls him downwards, but face upwards on the mat. The best of three "falls" wins.'

BRAWN

½ a salted pig's head, with the tongue	1 bayleaf
1 large onion	4 cloves
sprig of parsley, thyme, sage	1 teaspoon black peppercorns, whole

Wash and clean the pig's head, and put into a large saucepan covered with cold water. Bring to the boil, then pour off this water and rinse the pot. Put the head back into the saucepan with the other in-gredients, cover with fresh cold water, bring to the boil again, then simmer with the lid on for about 2–3 hours or until the bones pull out quite easily. Lift out the head, strain the stock and set it in a large bowl.

Take all the meat from the bones, remove fat and skin the tongue and chop the meat into small cubes. Put into a large dish or mould, slice the tongue into two and lay across the middle, covering it with the chopped pork. Take any fat from the stock (which will be jellied) and warm it enough for the jelly to melt, then carefully pour over the meat. Cover with foil, and when cool weight it lightly and chill. Turn out the next day and serve cut into thin slices with the following sauce.

Sauce for brawn

Mix together 2 tablespoons soft brown sugar, 3 tablespoons white wine vinegar, 4 tablespoons olive oil, 1 teaspoon made English mustard, a pinch of ground cloves or nutmeg, salt and pepper. Shake or stir very well before using.

Brawn can also be made with chicken and pork; rabbit and pork; beef flank and pork; or with all pork, using a mixture of lean and streaky meat. It is very like the French *fromage de tête*, and excellent for a good reasonably priced meal.

Grasmere wrestlers 'takin' hod', Grasmere Sports, 1897.

OAT CAKES or BISCUITS

The bracken is cut in the late autumn and used for bedding down the animals in place of straw. It was put on to a sledge or sled, or on small farms in a two-wheeled cart. The sledge was a common vehicle which was much easier to negotiate over the steeply sloping fields and it was only towards the end of the 19th century that the two-wheeled cart was used, four-wheeled carts being a rarity. In fact sleds are still to be found in the Lakeland dales; many farmers prefer them for there is no fear of them overturning. They are also used to transport hay and peat.

Packed lunches are often taken by the harvesters and consisted of oat cakes with cheese or cheese scones.

OAT CAKES or BISCUITS

Recipe kindly given by Mrs Jean Butterworth of White Moss House Hotel, Rydal Water, Grasmere.

225 g (8 oz) plain flour	75 g (3 oz) lard
225 g (8 oz) porridge oats	$\frac{1}{2}$ teaspoon salt
75 g (3 oz) castor sugar	$\frac{1}{2}$ teaspoon bicarbonate of soda
75 g (3 oz) margarine	3–4 tablespoons milk

Sieve the flour with the salt and the bicarbonate of soda. Then rub the fat into the mixed flour and oats and add the sugar. Gradually add a little milk at a time, mixing well until a firm dough is obtained. Roll out to about .5 cm ($\frac{1}{4}$ in) and cut into small rounds. Put on to a greased baking sheet and bake for about 10 minutes or until pale gold at 200°C (400°F) or gas mark 4. They are served buttered with soft cheese. Makes about 45.

CHEESE SCONES

225 g (8 oz) self-raising flour	50 g (2 oz) margarine
1 level teaspoon dry mustard	125 g (4 oz) grated hard cheese
powder	150 ml ($\frac{1}{4}$ pint) milk, preferably
a pinch of salt	sour, or buttermilk

Sift the flour, mustard and salt together, then rub in the fat until it resembles fine breadcrumbs. Add all but 1 large tablespoon of cheese and add the milk gradually to form a soft dough. Flour a board and turn out, then roll out to about 1.5 cm ($\frac{1}{2}$ in) thickness and cut either into triangles or 4 cm ($1\frac{1}{2}$ in) rounds. Put on to a lightly greased baking sheet, brush with a little milk and sprinkle the remaining cheese on top. Bake at 200°C (400°F) or gas mark 6 for 12–15 minutes. Makes about 20 scones.

Bringing down the bracken by sledge, c. 1890. Photographed by G. Abraham.

M EAT PASTY

Hunting in Lake country is somewhat different from other parts of the world; owing to the mountainous terrain where it would be impossible to ride a horse, it is done on foot and many miles can be covered in a day. As many as sixty were covered in a day by John Peel's hounds. The fox is a real danger to the young lambs and so most fox-hunting is done from necessity rather than purely for sport. It is a very democratic affair and usually organized by local farmers. However, it is a popular part of Lakeland life and many of its folk heroes were huntsmen, John Peel being the most famous. 'D'y ken John Peel with his coat so grey?' is sung all over the English-speaking world. His 'coat so grey' refers to the 'Skiddaw grey' or 'hodden' cloth which was woven locally from the undyed wool of the grey Herdwick sheep. John Peel was a typical farmer-huntsman and the song was written one night in 1832 by his friend John Wood-cock Graves. When he had finished writing it, Graves tossed the poem over to Peel saying: 'By gok John, thou'll be sung when both of us is run to earth!' John Peel was buried at Caldbeck in 1854 and it is said that when the funeral cortège passed the hound kennels they set up a chorus of howls deeply affecting all who heard it. The song was originally set to the music of 'Bonnie Annie', but the accompaniment and the air was re-arranged in 1868 by the organist at Carlisle Cathedral, William Metcalfe.

Others famous were Joe Borman, a huntsman with the Ullswater hounds from 1879 until 1924; Tommy Dobson who founded the Eskdale and Ennerdale Farmers' Hunt in 1857 and continued with it until 1910; and John Taylor of Baldhow, of whom it is said that his hounds killed fifty-six foxes in two years.

Hound trailing, which developed in the 19th century, is now almost as popular as wrestling (see page 44) and is one of the high spots of the Grasmere Sports Day. The hounds follow a false scent usually of aniseed and oil and the Hound Trailing Association which was formed in 1906 has laid down strict rules; speed is also taken into account. Hounds are taught to respond to signals, whistles and calls and the finish of a hound trail with the owners spurring their dogs on is an exciting and stirring event.

MEAT PASTY

This is a good thing to take on a hunt or hound trail, for it packs well and is nourishing. Make 450 g (1 lb) shortcrust pastry and roll it out thinly. Divide it into four to six rectangles about 20 cm (8 in) in length. Cover half of it with a mixture of chopped cooked lamb or beef finely chopped, mixed with finely chopped onion, a little chopped cooked potato and cooked carrot and a little mustard for beef or rowan jelly for lamb. Fill to within 2.5 cm (1 in) of the edges, then dampen the edges and fold over, pressing down well, make a slit on the top, brush with milk and bake in a moderate oven, 180°C (350°F) or gas mark 4, for 35–40 minutes. Serve warm or cold.

The end of the hunt by the Patterdale hounds, c. 1890. Photographed by G. Abraham.

CUMBERLAND SWEET PIE

Armathwaite Hall, in the north of Cumberland, was formerly a house of Benedictine nuns; during the Middle Ages it was frequently plundered and the nuns were wretchedly poor. Their income per head has been quoted as being £2 14s 0d per annum, as against over £24 per head for the monks of Furness Abbey. It was dissolved during the Reformation and much later became a private house. However, at about the turn of the century it became an hotel. It has extensive grounds with beautiful views of Bassenthwaite Lake.

There are but few packs of foxhounds followed by mounted huntsmen in this part of the world owing to the mountainous country, see page 48.

CUMBERLAND SWEET PIE

This traditional pie eaten at Christmas and the New Year is extremely good.

450 g (1 lb) shoulder lamb or mutton chops	pinch each of: ground cinnamon, mace, nutmeg
225 g (8 oz) each: raisins, currants and sultanas	½ teaspoon ground black pepper
150 g (5 oz) brown sugar	¼ teaspoon salt
juice of 1 large lemon and grated peel	2 eggs
50 g (2 oz) mixed chopped peel	2–3 tablespoons dark rum
	225 g (8 oz) flaky pastry (see page 120)

First trim the chops of bone and gristle and remove as much fat as you want. Put the chops into a saucepan, barely cover with water and bring to the boil. Simmer for about 20 minutes, drain, but reserve juice. Let the liquid cool and skim the fat from the top. Hard boil the eggs, run under cold water and shell, then cut into halves. Take a deep pie dish and layer all the ingredients for the pie, seasoning well. Add enough of the stock and the rum to barely cover. Dampen the edges of the dish and roll out the pastry to fit. Lay on, pressing down the edges and mark with a fork.

Bake at 200° (400°F) or gas mark 6 for 15 minutes, then lower the heat slightly to 180°C (350°F) or gas mark 4 and continue cooking for about a further 20 minutes. If the top is getting too brown, cover loosely with foil or greaseproof paper.

DAMSON GIN

This makes an excellent stirrup cup. Wash and pick the stalks from about 225 g (8 oz) sound damsons, then prick them all over with a large needle. Put into a large gin bottle and add half their amount of white sugar. Fill up with gin, leaving a small space between the gin and the cork. Cork tightly and leave for about three months, turning every day so that the sugar dissolves and the damsons are moved around. It becomes a most beautiful colour and is a potent drink! Sloes can also be done in this way to make sloe gin, and vodka can be used in place of gin if preferred. The damsons are very good to eat afterwards!

Meet of the Cumberland Foxhounds, master Sir Wilfred Lawson, at Armathwaite Hall, New Year's Day c. 1900.

RABBIT AND PORK PIE

Kirkstone Inn was a great place for 'Shepherds' Meet', see page 35, when great amounts of food and drink were consumed at the 'Merry Neet' afterwards, tatie-pot (page 35) and pies being traditional fare with many barrels of beer. A feature of these meetings is a contest to see who can pull the worst face, known in this part of the world as 'gurning' and a prize is given to the winner. The entire evening is one of great merriment. The inn is the sixth highest in England at 420 metres (1,468 feet) above sea-level and it is thought to have been built in 1840 for the refreshment of travellers. The Kirk-stone nearby resembles a roof: 'Whole Church-like frame, Gives to the savage Pass its name.' These Shepherds' Meets still take place but nowadays the location is in a more accessible place.

Wordsworth, who wrote 'Ode to the Pass of Kirkstone' was fond of walking up to the Kirkstone Pass and his sister Dorothy records in her Journal of April 1802: 'William finished his poem ["The Cock is Crowing"] before we got to the foot of Kirkstone ... There we ate our dinner. The walk up Kirkstone was very interesting. The Becks among the rocks were all alive. Wm. showed me the little mossy streamlet which he had loved when he saw its bright green track in the snow.'

The Kirkstone Pass winds up from Troutbeck and part of it used to be called 'The Struggle' in the days of four-in-hands and pack-ponies. A tourist wrote in the visitors' book at the inn in the last century:

'He surely is an arrant ass,
Who pays to ride up Kirkstone Pass,
He'll find in spite of all their talking
He'll have to walk, and pay for walking.'

RABBIT AND PORK PIE

This is delicious hot or cold; when the latter it will be jellied. Chicken can also be used.

225 g (8 oz) shortcrust pastry made from 225 g (8 oz) plain flour and 125 g (4 oz) margarine, 3–4 tablespoons iced water	125 g (4 oz) sausagemeat, optional, or 2 hard-boiled eggs
	1 medium onion, sliced
	1 tablespoon chopped parsley
1 jointed rabbit	pinch of powdered thyme
225 g (8 oz) streaky pork or bacon	$\frac{1}{4}$ teaspoon ground nutmeg
	salt and pepper

First make the pastry and leave to rest in a cold place while preparing the pie. Soak the rabbit joints in salted water for about 2 hours, drain, then simmer for 1 hour in water to cover, or use cider if you like. Cool and take all the meat from the bones. Trim the pork of rind and any excess fat and cut it into cubes. Season the sausagemeat and roll into tiny balls or hard boil the eggs, run them under cold water, shell and slice them. Layer it all in a deep pie dish, with the herbs, finely sliced onion, nutmeg and seasoning, and use the sausagemeat balls or eggs to fill up spaces and the corners. Barely cover with the strained stock, dampen the edges and cover with the pastry, making a small slit on top. Bake at 200°C (400°F) or gas mark 6 for 20 minutes, then lower to 180°C (350°F) or gas mark 4 for a further 20–25 minutes. Serves 6.

Shepherd at Kirkstone House Inn in winter, c. 1890.

CHRISTMAS BREAD

Mrs Arthur Severn, née Ruskin Agnew, was a cousin of the writer John Ruskin (see page 31); the year be bought Brantwood on Coniston Lake in 1871, Miss Joanna Ruskin Agnew married Arthur Severn and came to live at Brantwood with Ruskin as her companion. During his long illness she nursed him, and for the last ten years of his life he lived in retirement at Brantwood in the loving care of the Severn family, to whom the property passed on his death in January 1900.

CHRISTMAS BREAD

A traditional yule loaf not unlike those made in Scandinavian countries.

800 g (1 lb 12 oz) plain flour
1 teaspoon salt
3 heaped tablespoons lard, about 75 g (3 oz)
25 g (1 oz) fresh yeast or 15 g (½ oz) dried
2 large eggs
300 ml (½ pint) mixed tepid milk and water

125 g (4 oz) each: currants and sultanas
175 g (6 oz) raisins
50 g (2 oz) chopped mixed peel
1 tablespoon warm black treacle
1 rounded teaspoon mixed spice
175 g (6 oz) sugar

See that all ingredients are at room temperature and that the mixing bowl is warm. Put the sifted flour and salt into the bowl and rub in the lard thoroughly. Put the yeast in a basin with a teaspoon of the sugar. Beat the eggs well and add the warm, not hot, milk and water so that it makes about 450 ml (¾ pint) in all. Pour this over the yeast and stir well, then leave it to work. After about 10 minutes pour it into a well in the middle of the flour and work into a dough. Scatter a little flour over the top of the ball of dough, cover and put into a warm place for about 30–40 minutes to rise. Or wrap entirely in a polythene bag.

Punch down and knead well, then add all the other ingredients mixing them in thoroughly. Cover again and leave to rise for about 2 hours in a warm place, then divide between two loaf tins which have been lightly greased and wrap again in a polythene bag or cover and leave for 20 minutes. Put into a preheated oven at 200°C (400°F) or gas mark 6 on the central shelf and bake for 20 minutes, then lower the heat to 180°C (350°F) or gas mark 4 for a further 50 minutes.

When the loaves are cooked, take from the oven and brush the tops over with a little warmed milk to give a glaze, then put back for about 3–5 minutes to set. Cool on a wire rack, and serve cold, cut into slices and buttered. It keeps well in a tin.

The Severn family ice-bound on Coniston Water, winter 1895.

GINGERBREAD

Bowness on Windermere was the centre of all kinds of winter activities during the 'Great Freeze' of 1894–5. The remarkable frost lasted until March and thousands of people came here to skate, to go on the ice yacht, to travel by horse sleigh (see page 58) and at least one carriage plied for hire between Bowness and Belle Isle. Excursion trains were run to cope with the crowds; hotels, guest houses and inns did a good trade. An almost carnival-like atmosphere prevailed: two bands played from time to time, one on an island, and there was even a police ice patrol to see that the many thousands of people kept order. There were glowing braziers, refreshment stalls and hot drink stands on the ice-bound lake and it is said that in most places the ice was over 23 cm (9 in) thick. Yet through it all the ferry boat still ran, breaking a channel through the ice from Ferry Nab to the Ferry Hotel. Mrs Richards the proprietress of the Old England Hotel put a tall electric lamp on the lawn, for the skating continued during the night.

'The whole interspace between the land and the island was powdered white from the innumerable iron heels of the skaters. Here, a pony jingling with its jangling sleigh bells dashed along ... A hurdy-gurdy man made music here, and yonder ... a brass band blew its best, and risked frozen lips and frost-bitten fingers in the process. Tea, one was reminded was obtainable here; oranges were possible there. Presently a great boat-sail was seen to belly to the wind, and an ice-boat slid past.'   Skating on Windermere, H. D. Rawnsley, 1851–1920.

GINGERBREAD

This is a rich traditional gingerbread, delicious on a winter's day.

450 g (1 lb) plain flour, sifted	150 ml ($\frac{1}{4}$ pint) milk
225 g (8 oz) soft brown sugar	225 g (8 oz) butter or margarine
1 level teaspoon bicarbonate soda	225 g (8 oz) black treacle (molasses)
$\frac{1}{2}$ teaspoon mixed spice	225 g (8 oz) golden syrup or corn syrup
2 rounded teaspoons ground ginger	3 eggs, well beaten
pinch of salt	1 tablespoon chopped crystallized ginger or peel, optional

Mix all the dry ingredients together. Warm the milk and dissolve the butter in it, add the black treacle and syrup and finally add the beaten eggs. Pour this into the dry ingredients and mix very well together. Add the chopped ginger or peel, if you are using it, and mix again well. Grease a square 23 cm (9 in) shallow tin and put the mixture into it. Smooth the top over evenly and bake at 180°C (350°F) or gas mark 4 for about 1 hour, but test with a thin skewer before taking from the oven. Leave for about 2–3 minutes, then take out of the tin and cool on a rack.

On Windermere during the 'Great Freeze', 1895.

SNOW PANCAKES

Many forms of transport were used during the extraordinary frost of 1895, and many activities such as ice hockey and curling were played. See also page 57.

SNOW PANCAKES

This is a traditional method of making pancakes, but the snow must be of the light powdery kind, not wet and heavy, for the results to be good.

4 heaped tablespoons self-raising flour, sifted
12 tablespoons milk
oil or butter for frying
1 level teaspoon salt
4 tablespoons powdery snow
jam for filling

Add the salt to the flour, then gradually add the milk beating all the time until the batter is smooth and creamy. Add the snow and beat again. Heat up a heavy pan and rub over with a little fat or oil, not too much, and pour in 1 quarter of the batter. Roll the pan around so that it spreads evenly and when the bottom is golden toss or turn with a spatula and cook the other side until golden. Drain on kitchen paper and make the other three pancakes. Fill with jam and roll up. Serve hot. Makes 4.

GINGER SCONES

The ginger can be omitted if you want plain treacle scones.

25 g (1 oz) butter or margarine   pinch of salt

225 g (8 oz) plain flour, sifted
25 g (1 oz) sugar
1 level teaspoon each: bicarbonate soda and cream of tartar
2 teaspoons ground ginger
1 rounded tablespoon warmed golden syrup
1 egg
a little milk

Rub the butter into the sifted flour, and add all the other dry ingredients. Warm the syrup and add that, then add the beaten egg and mix very well into a soft dough. Turn on to a floured surface and roll out to 1.5 cm ($\frac{1}{2}$ in) thickness and cut into rounds or triangles. Put on a lightly greased baking sheet and brush over with a little milk before baking at 200°C (400°F) or gas mark 6 for 10–15 minutes. Serve hot with butter or rum butter.

RUM BUTTER

This is traditional to both Cumberland and Westmorland. It is eaten with scones, on steamed puddings, with mince pies and Christmas pudding. See also page 55.

Westmorland method
Soften 225 g (8 oz) unsalted butter, but do not let it oil. Beat in about 450 g (1 lb) Barbados sugar, or as much as the butter will take. Add half a grated nutmeg, mixing well, then gradually stir in 4–5 tablespoons rum, again mixing well and not adding more than the mixture will take. Put into bowls and use when it is set.

Cumberland method uses the same ingredients, but the sugar, nutmeg and rum are first mixed, then the butter is melted, poured over and well mixed before putting into bowls.

Mr Joseph Crosthwaite driving across Windermere to Belle Isle in a sleigh, during the 'Great Freeze' of 1895.

CUMBRIAN BACON CASSEROLE

Together with sheep-farming, mining has been a traditional occupation for many centuries in the Lake District. There were mines at Keswick, see page 119, and copper mines at Coniston; working conditions were hard and often dangerous. The Greenside lead mine was one of the few mines to be worked almost continuously from the 16th century until 1962 when it was closed, although the main development took place in 1825. Before then it had been worked mostly near the surface, the ore being carried over the Sticks Pass to the smelting works at Stoneycroft Ghyll in Newlands, but in 1825 it was highly mechanized according to the standards of the day and made increasing profits. The principal ore was galena which when smelted gave about 80% lead and 12 ounces of silver per ton. In later years the smelting was done at the mine itself; the miners' huts are now used as a Youth Hostel. There is not very much mining done in this area now, but in 1971 a tungsten ore mine was reopened in Mosedale at the foot of Carrock Fell.

Protective clothing was unknown until the 20th century and the miners wore thick woollen trousers and long leather jackets. Instead of boots, which were expensive and difficult to dry out, they wore the traditional clogs lined with straw, sometimes without socks so that they could pour out the water and replace the wet straw with fresh. Clogs were worn by all classes from labourers to parsons, and often the wives preserved stocking heels by smearing them with melted pitch and then dipping them in turf ashes. The clogs had soles of alder wood and leather uppers, women's clogs having brass clasps and the men's iron. The wooden soles were shod with iron caulkers or 'corkers' and skilled cloggers worked in Kendal, Keswick and Ulverston. They are still being made today as they are preferred by some farmers for comfort and warmth.

CUMBRIAN BACON CASSEROLE

Recipe kindly given by Allen Cairns of the Swan Hotel, Thornthwaite, Keswick, noted for its food.

12 bacon chops approximately 1.6 kg (3½ lbs)	salt and pepper
	2 large chopped onions
225 g (8 oz) split green or yellow dried peas & orange lentils, mixed, soaked overnight	450 g (1 lb) carrots, sliced
	1 small head celery, roughly chopped
125 g (4 oz) butter, margarine or oil	1 large clove garlic
	850 ml (1½ pints) approx stock
1 teaspoon mixed dried herbs	fresh parsley for garnish

Soak the dried peas and lentils in cold water to cover overnight. Trim the bacon chops of any rind and fat. Heat the butter and soften the onions, carrots and celery in it, then add the drained pulses, herbs and seasoning. Barely cover with stock, bring to the boil and simmer for 1½–2 hours on top of the stove.

Halfway through cooking time put the chops on a rack in a roasting pan and cook at 170°C (325°F) or gas mark 3 for about 35 minutes or until lightly crisp. Arrange on top of the vegetables (the stock should have evaporated in the cooking and been absorbed) and return to the oven for 15 minutes. Garnish with parsley and serve with baked potatoes. Enough for 6.

Turbine House and pipe track at Greenside Mine, c. 1900.

BAKED STUFFED HADDOCK

The first graphite, or plumbago, ever discovered in England was found in the Seathwaite Valley on the side of the mountain Seathwaite Fell in Borrowdale near Keswick around 1500. The shepherds who found it after a violent storm had uprooted large trees tearing away the subsoil thought it was coal, but found it wouldn't burn, although it made a good sheep marking. Its value was soon appreciated and the mines were taken over by the government who transported the graphite to London by armed stagecoach. Although useful for making a primitive form of pencil, it was used also for medicinal purposes but its chief use during Queen Elizabeth I's reign was for the manufacture of cannon balls. The local name for it was 'wad' and even today a graphite pencil is often called a 'wad' pencil locally. German miners were brought over to work the mines which were closed during the Civil War, but reopened again in the early 18th century when much stealing and smuggling of the 'wad' took place; so much so that the offence was punishable by hard labour or transportation. The mine output was already dwindling by 1833 and it was finally closed between 1885 and 1890 after spasmodic working.

The mill in the photograph was a woollen mill in 1800, but was taken over for the manufacture of pencils in 1810. Charles Greenwood, the grandfather of the present director ran the mill with seven employees around 1908 and it has remained in the family ever since, although it is now part of the Twinlock group, but it is some years since local graphite has been used. There is an interesting small museum west of the new factory, by the old factory near the Greta river.

BAKED STUFFED HADDOCK

Although not great fish eaters, the favourite sea-fish of the Lakelands is haddock, often served fried or baked. Other white fish can be used in place of haddock if preferred.

900 g (2 lb) fresh haddock fillets, skinned	4 tablespoons single cream salt and freshly ground white pepper

For the stuffing

125 g (4 oz) fresh white breadcrumbs	25 g (1 oz) melted butter or margarine
1 tablespoon chopped parsley	1 small egg
$\frac{1}{4}$ teaspoon dried thyme or fennel	salt and pepper
1 lemon	

Lightly butter an ovenproof dish, then lay half the fillets in it. Make the stuffing by mixing the breadcrumbs, parsley and thyme or fennel together, then cut the lemon in half and add the finely grated rind and juice from one half. Bind with the egg and finally add the rest of the butter and season to taste. Lay this on top of the fillets evenly, then cover with the remaining fillets. Slice the rest of the lemon thinly and place over the top, season with the salt and white pepper, then add the cream. Cover with foil and bake at 180°C (350°F) or gas mark 4 for about 30 minutes. Serves 4.

The Cumberland Pencil Company Mill, Keswick, c. 1890.

OATMEAL BREAD

Brush-making was another industry for which Kendal was known, see also page 67. The brushes were made from the finest imported boar bristles and the symbol of the black hog still hangs today over Blackhall House, Stricklandgate, now the offices of Messrs Thompson & Matthews. Blackhall was a private mansion built in the 17th century and was the home of the Wilson family for hundreds of years. It became a brush factory in 1869.

The photograph illustrates the child labour still being used at this date. Oatmeal was still used a lot at this time for both bread and cakes.

OATMEAL BREAD

300 ml (½ pint) scalded milk	25 g (1 oz) fresh yeast or 12 g
300 ml (½ pint) water	(½ oz) dried
125 g (4 oz) golden syrup	700 g (1½ lb) plain strong flour
½ teaspoon salt	125 g (4 oz) rolled oats

Cool the milk to 26°C (80°F) and heat the water to lukewarm; pour both into a slightly warmed basin and add the syrup and salt. Crumble the yeast into this and stir until it is dissolved. Sift the flour and when the yeast has worked a little add 450 g (1 lb) and beat with a wooden spoon until smooth. Cover and stand in a warm place until double its bulk, about 2–3 hours. Then stir in the remaining flour and the oatmeal. Knead until the dough is smooth and elastic and put into a lightly greased warm basin, cover and leave again until double the size. Then draw down the sides with the fingers towards the centre and punch down. Cover again and leave for 1 hour, then divide into two and put into 2 lightly greased 900 g (2 lb) loaf tins. Brush the tops with melted butter, cover and leave for about half an hour. Then bake at 190–200°C (375–400°F) or gas mark 5–6 for 20 minutes, then lower the heat to 180°C (350°F) or gas mark 4 for a further 40 minutes or until well browned.

Note: the proving time is shortened a little if the dough is put into a lightly greased large polythene bag and tied up.

OATEN DATE CRISPS

125 g (4 oz) wholewheat flour	2 tablespoons water
175 g (6 oz) rolled oats	2 teaspoons lemon juice
225 g (8 oz) margarine	25 g (1 oz) soft brown sugar
225 g (8 oz) chopped stoned dates	pinch of ground cinnamon

Mix the flour and oats together, then rub in the fat. Turn out on to a lightly floured surface and knead until smooth. Cut into half and press one half into a greased 18 cm (7 in) square cake tin. Simmer the chopped dates with the water until soft, cool, stir in the lemon juice, sugar and cinnamon and spread this over the dough, then cover with the other half of the dough. Smooth the top over and bake at 180°C (350°F) or gas mark 4 for 25 minutes. Cut while warm into slices, and leave to cool in the tin. Apples can also be used, in which case increase sugar.

Boar Sign brush factory, Kendal, c. 1910.

KENDAL WIGS

Kendal was a great centre for weaving, and skilled weavers from Flanders and other parts of Europe were encouraged to come to England by letters of protection granted by Edward III and later by Richard II for master weavers and apprentices to settle in many wool manufacturing towns. Kendal cotton was spotted by hand and dyed in a variety of colours. In 1582 William Camden wrote of Kendal: 'The tenter grounds on the sides of the little hills resemble the growth of vine orchards in Spain, having many coloured cloths upon them ...' This dye was also used to colour 'Pace-Eggs', see page 23. Christmas was another festival with many traditions in food: apart from the usual puddings and pies, there was Cumberland Sweet Pie, page 51, rum butter, page 59, and Kendal wigs and 'Double Sweaters', the latter being teacakes with two thick layers of sugared currants sandwiched between them. Spiced ale was also popular, as well as damson wine and punch, pages 20 and 91.

KENDAL WIGS

These were originally a yeasted bun made from 450 g (1 lb) flour, 40 g (1½ oz) lard, 40 g (1½ oz) brown sugar, 25 g (1 oz) yeast, a pinch of salt, some caraway seeds or currants all mixed to a soft and elastic dough with milk or water, left to prove and baked in small buns in a moderate oven 180°C (350°F) or gas mark 4 for about half an hour. They were split and spread with rum butter while still warm. However today when yeast is not so much used, an alternative recipe is:

75 g (3 oz) butter	2 teaspoons caraway seeds or 25 g
225 g (8 oz) self-raising flour, sifted	(1 oz) currants
	1 egg
25 g (1 oz) sugar	a little milk

Mr R. Dixon, the last hand-loom weaver, Salmon's Yard, Highgate, Kendal.

Rub the butter into the sifted flour, and add the sugar and caraway seeds or currants. Mix to a soft dough with the beaten egg and a little milk, adding the latter gradually. Put into greased patty-tins and bake at 220°C (425°F) or gas mark 7 for about 20 minutes. They are good eaten with mulled elderberry or damson wine, or with warm beer. Makes about 20.

DAMSON PICKLE

The damsons from the Lyth Valley southwest of Kendal are famous for their excellence.

700 g (1½ lb) sound, ripe damsons	1 teaspoon whole cloves
	1 level teaspoon cinnamon, or small piece
350 g (12 oz) sugar	
600 ml (1 pint) white malt vinegar	1 tablespoon pickling spice

Prick each damson with a fork or large needle and put into a big bowl. Boil together the sugar, spices and vinegar and pour over the damsons. Cover and leave overnight. Next day drain off liquid, reboil and pour over again, leave overnight and repeat once more. Then boil all together for 5 minutes gently keeping the fruit whole. Put into warm jars and tie down. This is excellent with cold mutton, game or cheese.

DAMSON CHUTNEY

This is made by cooking together 1 kg (2 lb 3 oz) stoned damsons with 450 g (1 lb) peeled and cored, chopped apples, 450 g (1 lb) brown sugar, 225 g (8 oz) chopped onions, a pinch of ginger, mixed spice, pickling spice and salt with 600 ml (1 pint) malt vinegar for about 1 hour. Bottle and seal while hot. Makes about 2.3 kg (5 lb).

CUMBRIAN APPLE PUDDING

The making of a 'swill' or 'spelk' (from the old Norse word spelker – splinter) is another traditional Lake District craft which still continues, albeit in limited quantities. It is an ancient craft with records going back to the 16th century. Swills are made from oak poles which are split into pieces then boiled in water to make them pliable. They are further split and then shaved into strips on a swiller's 'horse' on which the swiller sits astride. While the wood is boiling the oval rims are made from hazel or ash withies, these too being boiled for a few minutes, then shaped into oval frames and nailed. This is woven with short strong cross pieces, and taws, the longer pieces. So fine is the craftsmanship that it is said that the best swills will hold water. They are made in various sizes and are used in farming, coal-mining, charcoal-making, on board ship and of course for holding wood logs or coal in houses. Mr Charlie Airey of Storth still makes them, selecting his own timber and using the family 'horse' which has been handed down in his family for over two hundred years.

CUMBRIAN APPLE PUDDING

This is an unusual pudding, good to taste, and made from the excellent apples grown nearby.

175 g (6 oz) fresh white breadcrumbs	1 tablespoon warmed golden syrup
75 g (3 oz) grated suet	175 g (6 oz) grated cooking apples
125 g (4 oz) white sugar	grated rind of 1 lemon
1 rounded teaspoon baking powder	2 medium eggs, beaten
	4–5 tablespoons milk

1 level teaspoon mixed: ground cloves and cinnamon

Mix together all the dry ingredients, then add the golden syrup, the grated apples, the beaten eggs and finally add the milk gradually until a soft dough is formed. Turn into a lightly greased basin, cover with foil or greaseproof paper, tie down and steam over boiling water for 2 hours. Serve hot turned out on to a warmed dish, with cream or fresh custard. Enough for 4–6.

RUM DOG

This curiously named steamed pudding is traditional to these parts and eaten with a generous portion of rum butter spread on top. These puddings were great 'filler-uppers'.

225 g (8 oz) self-raising flour	75 g (3 oz) Valencia raisins, stoned and soaked in 2–3 tablespoons rum or half rum and half black tea
125 g (4 oz) shredded suet	
150 ml ($\frac{1}{4}$ pint) water, approx	

Mix all the ingredients except the water together, then add the water gradually until a soft dough is formed. You might need a little more water, but add it gradually as the mixture should not be too wet. Butter a large piece of foil, or flour a pudding cloth, put the mixture in and tie up loosely to allow for expansion. Steam over boiling water for about 1 hour, and to serve, cut into thick slices while hot and put a generous spoonful of rum butter on each portion. Serves 4–6.

Making a 'swill' basket, Furness Fells, c. 1890.

CHARCOAL BURNER'S WOOD PIGEON

Charcoal burning was once an important industry in the Furness area, as it was the most effective fuel for smelting. The Cistercian monks of Furness Abbey had 'colepittes' in the woods of Low Furness to supply the abbey with enough charcoal to smelt the red haematite ores, but by the 16th century the woods were so depleted that the ore had to be transported to small 'bloomery hearths' throughout the High Furness Fells. It took five tons of wood to produce one ton of charcoal, so it was necessary to keep a watchful eye to prevent deforestation. The coppices were cleared of saplings about five or six inches in diameter between November and April when the sap was minimal, only oak trees being left until the spring to allow the bark to be peeled more easily. The summer months were utilized by cutting, peeling and sorting the wood, the larger trunks being sent to the bobbin mills.

The charcoal making process, which continued until 1937 in the Lake District (for charcoal was an important ingredient of gunpowder), changed little over the centuries. First a shallow circular pit between twenty and thirty feet was dug and a stake or 'motty peg' set up in the middle. Around the stake pieces of wood about a yard long were piled concentrically, beehive-shaped about six feet tall. This was then covered in bracken or grass to check the air current which would cause the wood to burn too fiercely. This pile was also protected from winds by a series of movable interlaced wooden screens (see photograph). The middle stake was taken out and a piece of glowing charcoal put there instead and damped down with an earth sod. Once lit it required constant attention lest it collapse and any sign of a flame had to be damped or smothered with wet turf, (as in the photograph) or water. This 'coaling' process could take between one to three days and great skill was needed on the part of the collier to see

how the pit was progressing. When this stage was over, a 'saying' of water was thrown over to create steam to cool the charcoal, which was left to get cold before putting into sacks.

The men stayed on the site during this time, living in conical wigwam-like huts made of wood and turf sods about eight foot high which they built themselves and held two people. Food was brought to them by farmers' wives or daughters, but they were not averse to cooking over their fire the odd game bird or rabbit that might come their way.

CHARCOAL BURNER'S WOOD PIGEON

Chicken or small game birds such as snipe or woodcock can also be cooked this way. Clean the bird or birds and split them in half. Season well then rub all over with butter or oil and sprinkle with some chopped mixed herbs. Cook over hot, but not flaming charcoal, cut side downwards to start with, for about 20–25 minutes, turning at least twice and brushing several times with melted butter. They are ready if when pricked with a fork the juices run clear and are not pink or red. They are very good served with damson pickle, page 67, or apple sauce, page 32. Allow 1 pigeon per person.

Burning wood to make charcoal, Winster, c. 1900.

BORROWDALE TEA BREAD

Farming is still the main industry in this district and sheep the most important livestock. Possibly this old man was a shepherd once, who in later years tended his cottage garden. Borrowdale has the Bowder Stone, a giant lump of rock, sixty-two feet long and thirty-six feet high, which lies like a ship upon its keel. It is eighty-nine feet in circumference and weighs nearly 2,000 tons. There is a kind of ladder resting against the side and from its top there is a fine view. Nearby are the Falls of Lodore about which Robert Southey wrote a poem called 'The Cataract of Lodore', when he lived nearby at Greta Hall, Keswick (see page 19).

'Here it comes sparkling,
And there it lies darkling;
Now smoking and frothin'
Its tumult and wrath in,
Till in this rapid race
On which it is bent,
It reaches the place
Of its steep descent.'

BORROWDALE TEA BREAD

Recipe from *Lakeland Cookery* by kind permission of Jean Seymour.

450 g (1 lb) mixed currants, raisins and sultanas
12 tablespoons strong milkless tea
175 g (6 oz) soft brown sugar
1 large egg, beaten

25 g (1 oz) butter or margarine, melted
250 g (9 oz) plain flour, sifted
½ teaspoon bicarbonate of soda
a pinch of salt

Soak the fruit overnight in the tea, then the next day stir in the sugar. Add the well beaten egg and the melted butter. Fold in the sifted flour mixed with the bicarbonate of soda and the salt. Mix well, so that it is all well blended, then put into a lightly greased 450 g (1 lb) loaf tin and bake in a moderate oven, 180°C (350°F) or gas mark 4, for 1½–2 hours. Leave in the tin for about 5 minutes, then turn out and cool on a wire rack. Serve sliced and spread with butter.

A summer evening near Borrowdale, c. 1870.

R OAST GOOSE

Geese were usually kept on country farms for not only did they provide meat, but also fine large eggs and downy feathers which were used to stuff mattresses and pillows. Geese are territorial birds and make good watch-dogs, honking loudly at the approach of strangers. If the sheep-dog was out on the mountains rounding up sheep, the farmer's wife could rest assured that the property would be well guarded.

Fat geese or fat capons were the Christmas birds and they could be kept around the yard and fattened on household scraps and corn. With a large piece of boiled bacon they made a good feast. 'Green' geese, the young ones fed on pasture were traditionally served at Michaelmas and this is thought to have come from the habit of farm tenants when paying their Michaelmas rent of giving the landlord a stubble (fat) goose and having a green one themselves. These young geese were seldom stuffed since it was thought to spoil the delicate flavour, but they were always served with apple sauce (page 32) when hot, and in the Lake country with pickled damsons (page 67) and the bacon when cold.

'And when the tenants come to pay their quarter's rent
They bring some fowls at Midsummer,
A dishe of fishe in Lent;
At Christmas a capon, at Michaelmas a goose ...'   *Old country rhyme.*

ROAST GOOSE

1 goose about 4.5 kg (10 lb)	*For the stuffing*
flour	450 g (1 lb) onions
pepper and salt	125 g (4 oz) breadcrumbs
2–3 tablespoons oil or butter	chopped liver of the bird
600 ml (1 pint) giblet stock	25 g (1 oz) butter, melted
	2 teaspoons crushed sage
	pinch of ground nutmeg
	salt and pepper

First put on the giblets, except the liver, well covered with water, salt and pepper to taste. Bring to the boil, and simmer gently for about 1 hour, then cool and remove any fat from the top. Make the stuffing by peeling and quartering the onions, then cooking them in boiled salted water for not more than 10–15 minutes. Strain and chop them. Put into a basin and add all the other stuffing ingredients, mixing well. Put the mixture into the crop and body of the bird and secure well.

Put the trussed bird into a roasting tin, and if fat prick all over lightly. Rub it with flour, pepper and salt, then pour over the oil or rub the butter over. Cover with foil, loosely and roast a 200°C (400°F) or gas mark 6 for 20 minutes per 450 g (1 lb) and 20 minutes over. Baste well every half an hour. Half an hour before it is ready take off the foil to allow it to brown. Pour off excess fat and add the giblet stock to make the gravy. Boil up to reduce. Serves 10.

Driving the geese and goslings, c. 1890.

GRASMERE GINGERBREAD

Sarah Nelson was a remarkable woman and her fame still continues because her original gingerbread recipe is still being baked at the tiny shop which holds only about three customers at a time in Grasmere village. This small dwelling was a school run by the church from 1660 to 1854 and when new premises were built it was given to the newly widowed Sarah Nelson and her two daughters to live in. Tragically one daughter died when eighteen years old from tuberculosis and to make ends meet in 1855 Sarah Nelson started making her own variety of gingerbread and selling it to travellers. It is not in the least like any gingerbread you have ever eaten, either in texture or taste, for it is flat with a crisp biscuit-like texture, the taste being redolent with spice. The recipe is still being made, but it is a strictly guarded secret and reposes in the National Westminster Bank. Many have tried to emulate it, but it proves elusive.

Mrs Nelson continued to make and sell her gingerbread until her death in 1904 when the now flourishing business was carried on by two nieces who sold it to an Uncle and his wife, Gerald and Margaret Wilson, who still maintain the tradition. Gerald Wilson was previously a joiner, but now does all the baking and his wife and daughter serve in the original shop which is open and packed with customers, from April until November. Nearby is Dove Cottage, one-time home of William and Dorothy Wordsworth, and later lived in by Thomas De Quincy, so many of the visitors to Dove Cottage go home with their package of the original Grasmere gingerbread. This is also served at the Grasmere Sports, see page 43, and at the annual Grasmere rushbearing ceremony which takes place on the Sunday nearest to St Oswald's Day, 5 August. Six young girls in green and white tunics carry a linen rush-sheet, hand spun in 1891 by a Mrs Wilson and handwoven in Keswick, to commemorate the days when the damp earthen church floors were strewn with rushes. There is dancing around the decorated Maypole as well.

GRASMERE GINGERBREAD

None of the recipes given approximate to the genuine article but my experiments lead me to believe that it was, and still is, made either with a fine oatmeal or whole wheat flour. Here is my version which is very like the real thing.

Mix together 225 g (8 oz) either of fine oatmeal or whole wheat flour, 2 rounded teaspoons ground ginger, ½ teaspoon each of bicarbonate of soda and cream of tartar. When well mixed beat in 1 rounded tablespoon golden syrup, 225 g (8 oz) pale brown soft sugar and 125 g (4 oz) butter all gently melted together. This should bind it dryly. Do not add any liquid. Press into a 20 cm (8 in) shallow, square tin firmly, and bake at 170°C (325°F) or gas mark 3 for 50 minutes. Leave in the tin until cold, but mark into squares or fingers as it is cooling.

Mrs Sarah Nelson outside her gingerbread shop, Grasmere, 1890s.

WESTMORLAND SHIPPED HERRINGS

The market at Kendal was first granted in 1189 by Richard I for the sale of corn, fruit, vegetables and fish. Kendal was also famous for its wool trade from the 13th century and produced the Kendal green cloth: 'The Kendal archers all in green' ... Under its coat of arms is the motto: Pannus mihi panis – wool is my bread. It is also well known for snuff making, brushes (see page 64) and mint cake (page 107). Katharine Parr the eldest child of Sir Thomas Parr, Baron of Kendal and Controller of the Household to Henry VIII, was born at Kendal Castle in 1512 and she became Henry VIII's last wife.

Kendal has long had a vigorous life much of which centred around its markets, for pack-horses brought produce over the fells and rivers. In 1754 post-chaises were introduced and two years later the first stage-coaches replaced the pack-horse trains. In 1762 the first stagecoach from London, called the 'Flying Machine on Steel Springs', was introduced and this led to a number of good coaching inns. Another important event was in 1767 when it was first lighted with oil lamps, employing a paid lamp-lighter. It is still a lively town with many good pubs and restaurants, but it would be hard to beat a Christmas dinner served at the King's Arms in 1841. The jockey John Singleton's father had been innkeeper of that establishment and he was born there in 1736. He won the first St Leger in 1776, and jockeyed the famous horse Eclipse in all his races.

'A dinner served at the famous old Inn, the King's Arms, Kendal. The good lady served at Christmas at the Commercial Travellers' Association, a pie containing: 2 fat geese, 2 large turkeys, 4 fowl, 2 pheasants, 4 geese, 2 hares, 4 rabbits, 3 tongues, 8 pounds of beef steaks and ham. The circumference of the pie was seven feet and the depth 10 inches, while the weight was five stone and eight pounds.'   London Standard, 1841.

The Fish Market at Kendal, c. 1890s.

WESTMORLAND SHIPPED HERRINGS

Adapted from an 18th-century recipe. Remove the head, backbones, tails and fins from 4 fresh herrings. Poach the herring roes gently in boiling salted water. Then chop them and mix with 1 tablespoon soft, fresh, white breadcrumbs, 1 teaspoon anchovy essence, 2 teaspoons minced onion, and 1 tablespoon melted butter, some salt and pepper and a pinch of nutmeg.

Stuff the herrings with this and secure them. Place in a fireproof dish with a nut of butter on each. Bake in a moderate oven, 180°C (350°F) or gas mark 4, for 30 minutes and serve hot with the following sauce. If there are no roes, use 2 mashed hard-boiled eggs instead.

MUSTARD BUTTER SAUCE

Gently heat 75 g (3 oz) butter which has been mixed with 1 rounded teaspoon mustard powder, $\frac{1}{2}$ teaspoon anchovy essence and 1 teaspoon of lemon juice. Let it just come to foaming point, then pour over the fish or serve separately. Enough for 4.

CUMBERLAND HAM WITH CUMBERLAND SAUCE

The Windermere ferry at this time was propelled by oars, and often the passengers had to help in the rowing. This barge dated from the 18th century and steam did not replace it until about 1870, see page 83.

The Ferry Inn had large stabling attached, and behind the inn was a bowling green where annual sports were held. From about 1818 the Ferry Inn was a rendezvous for the yachtsmen, as the craft for the regattas and races usually met off the inn. There were races for fishermen's boats, innkeepers' boats and one for gentlemen. Afterwards excellent dinners were served at the inn which was patronized by the 'gentry and quality of the district'. It was pulled down in 1882.

CUMBERLAND HAM WITH CUMBERLAND SAUCE

Traditionally this sweet and delicate-tasting ham was boiled, but it can also be baked either wrapped in foil or a flour and water paste.

1 ham approx 4.5 kg (10 lb) soaked in cold water overnight	*For the sauce*
2 sprigs parsley	225 g (8 oz) redcurrant jelly
pepper	6 tablespoons port wine or elderberry wine
1 teaspoon brown sugar	grated rind and juice of 1 lemon
a squeeze of lemon juice	and 1 large orange
	a pinch of made mustard

Take the ham out of the soaking water, scrape the skin, put into a large saucepan with the parsley, pepper, sugar and lemon and cover with cold water. Bring to the boil, skim, then simmer gently, for 20 minutes per 450 g (1 lb) and for 20 minutes over, but it is wise to check before the last 20 minutes as different hams vary in cooking time. Leave to cool slightly in the liquid then lift out on to a large dish and strip off the skin levelling up the fat nicely if it is uneven. Cut across the fat with a sharp knife to make a diamond pattern and top with a mixture of dry breadcrumbs (50 g or 2 oz) mixed with half the amount of soft brown sugar and a teaspoon of made mustard to bind it. Spread this over the top and press down well. It can be further garnished with cherries, pineapple, apricots, or oranges and lemon slices. The garnish can be served cold cut into thin slices, or it can be baked with a little of the ham stock, covered with a piece of foil in a hot oven, 210°C (425°F) or gas mark 7, for about 30–40 minutes.

CUMBERLAND SAUCE

This sauce keeps very well in a screw-top jar so it is wise to make at least double the quantity you need and keep it in the fridge. It is also good with pork or game. Bring the jelly and wine to the boil and simmer until it is reduced by a quarter. Then add the other ingredients, mix well, bring to the boil and serve separately either hot or cold.

The Ferry Inn and Windermere ferry, c. 1860.

WINDERMERE FRUIT CAKE

The first steam ferry was about 1870; the boiler and engine were on one side and this made the ferry list to that side. On one occasion the wire broke and the ferry drifted towards Storrs, so after that a guide rope was added. The public ferry across Windermere is thought to have been in existence for about five hundred years and in 1635 there is an account of a ferry capsizing with nearly fifty people being drowned. See also page 80.

top over. Put into an oven preheated to 180°C (350°F) or gas mark 4 for half an hour, then reduce the heat to 150°C (300°F) or gas mark 2 and cook for a further 2 hours, but test with a skewer before taking from the oven. Let it cool for a little while before taking from the tin and cooling on a wire rack.

WINDERMERE FRUIT CAKE

This is a rich fruit cake which keeps very well in a tin.

175 g (6 oz) butter
175 g (6 oz) soft brown sugar
4 medium eggs
225 g (8 oz) plain flour, sifted
   with a pinch of salt

125 g (4 oz) each currants and
   raisins
175 g (6 oz) sultanas
50 g (2 oz) each: glacé cherries
   and chopped mixed peel
50 g (2 oz) blanched, chopped
   almonds
1 teaspoon mixed spice

Cream the butter and sugar until light and well mixed. Add the beaten eggs alternately with a small spoonful of flour, then gradually add the rest of the flour and finally the spice, fruit and the nuts. Mix very well.
   Put into a greased and lined 20 cm (8 in) cake tin and smooth the

The steam ferry carrying horses and coach on the Red Rover Tour to Furness Abbey from Windermere, c. 1870s.

ROAST WILD DUCK with PORT WINE

Rothay *was the last paddle steamer to be built for the Windermere United Steam Yacht Company and the Windermere Iron Steam Boat Company. She was built at Newby Bridge in 1866 by the Lancaster Ship Building Company. Her length overall was 105 feet, beam 15 feet and draught 6 feet 6 inches. The first steamer on the lake was* The Lady of the Lake, *a wooden paddle steamer launched in 1846, to cope with all the thousands of tourists who flocked to the district, but she ran aground in 1861 and was wrecked. Then an iron paddle steamer* The Firefly *was launched by a rival company in 1850 but she collided with* The Lady of the Lake. *In 1858 the two companies amalgamated and built the* Rothay. *After this* The Swan *an iron screw vessel was built by T. B. Seath of Rutherglen in 1869 and she continued in service until 1938. The Furness Railways took over the United Company and they were incorporated into the London Midland and Scottish group which launched two motor vessels, the* Teal II *and the* Swan II. *Today British Rail's Sealink operates the steamer service which runs daily during the summer.*

ROAST WILD DUCK with PORT WINE

This is an 18th-century recipe and can also be used for widgeon or teal, but as they are smaller birds they will need only about half the cooking time. A medium-sized mallard duck will make a good meal for two people with a few leftovers which are good for soup with the carcase.

2 wild duck about 1 kg (2.3 lb) each
4–6 rashers streaky bacon
2 tablespoons dripping or 4 tablespoons oil
salt and freshly ground black pepper
juice of 1 lemon
pinch of cayenne pepper
8 tablespoons port
1 teaspoon mushroom ketchup
2 tablespoons brandy

Wild duck should be dusted with black pepper and hung for at least 4 days in a cool place after plucking and before cooking. Cover the breasts with the bacon rashers, put into a roasting tin, add the dripping or oil and cook in a moderate to hot oven, 190–200°C (375–400°F) or gas mark 5–6 for 40 minutes, basting at least once during this time. Then remove the bacon and roll it (it can be used as a garnish) and let the breasts brown a little for about 7 minutes. Remove from the oven and put on to a warmed serving dish, score along the breastbone two or three times and sprinkle over the lemon juice, salt and pepper. Cover with foil and keep hot.

Pour off any excess fat from the roasting tin and scrape down the sides. Add the port, mushroom ketchup and cayenne pepper. Stir well, boil up and let it reduce slightly. Warm up the brandy in a ladle, set it alight and add to the sauce. Pour this at once over the ducks and serve with a watercress salad and some thin, crisp fried potatoes.

You can joint the ducks before putting them on the dish which does make serving easier. Enough for 4 and any cold duck is delicious served either with rowan jelly, page 20, or Cumberland sauce, page 80.

The paddle steamer Rothay, *Bowness Bay, c. 1870.*

CONISTON PUDDING

Gondola, *a steam passenger barge commissioned by the Furness Railway Company, was launched on Coniston Water's west shore in 1859. She was built in sections in Liverpool and transported by rail and cart for assembly at Coniston Hall. Her hull of Low Moor wrought iron is 85 foot long with a beam of 14′ 2″ and she draws 4′ 6″ at the stern, but only one foot at the stem, for close in-shore work. She had a V-shaped twin cylinder 16 hp engine, which powered a four-blade bronze propellor with a four-foot span to achieve a cruising speed of ten knots. There are two saloons, one of which is ornately decorated in blue and white with luxurious cushions and carpets. For eight years she made regular journeys between Waterhead and Lake Bank as well as cruises around the lake, and was greatly admired by John Ruskin, Thomas Carlyle and Arthur Ransome. Her activities covered five reigns and in 1906 alone she carried 22,445 passengers.*

Gondola was retired as late as 1940, and in 1944 her engine and boiler were removed to power a sawmill at Ulverston. Gondola descended to being simply a houseboat. Then in the winter of 1963–4 she was washed ashore in a bad storm and was condemned to be broken up. However, she was bought by Mr Arthur Hatton who saved some of the lovely interior fittings and half-submerged the boat to preserve her hull in the south end of Coniston Water.

The National Trust showed great interest in Gondola, and in 1977 refloated the hulk and brought her ashore at Coniston Hall where she was stripped and cleaned down. Plans for her restoration are now underway to save this graceful and unique reminder of the elegant past, and a National Trust Gondola Appeal Fund is open at Barclays Bank Ltd, *Bridge End, Coniston, Cumbria. It is to be hoped that she will be saved in the near future, once again to steam around the lake with passengers.*

CONISTON PUDDING

This is more of a tart than a pudding and is very good served warm or cold. It can also be made in small individual tins for a tea-time delicacy.

For the pastry	*For the filling*
225 g (8 oz) flour	1 egg
125 g (4 oz) butter	1 tablespoon castor sugar
1 tablespoon icing sugar	$\frac{1}{4}$ teaspoon grated nutmeg
1 egg	150 ml ($\frac{1}{4}$ pint) creamy milk, hot
	25 g (1 oz) each: raisins, currants and chopped candied peel

Make the pastry by rubbing the fat into the flour, then adding the sugar and the beaten egg. Roll into a ball, leave to rest and line a 20 cm (8 in) flan dish with it, crimping the edges. Lightly prick the bottom with a fork and brush with a little of the beaten egg. Beat in the sugar and nutmeg with rest of the beaten egg, then the hot milk and the fruit; pour this into the pastry case and bake at 180°C (350°F) or gas mark 4 for 50 minutes. Serves 4–6.

Gondola on Coniston Water, c. 1880s.

BAKED SALMON with CUCUMBER SAUCE

Colonel Ridehalgh of Fell Foot was a prominent yachting man and the Fairy Queen *was his first steamer. Later, in 1879, he was to commission T. B. Seath of Rutherglen to build him another steam yacht called the* Britannia *which can be seen moored in the photograph on page 93. The* Britannia *cost £12,000 to build, but was sold in 1907 to the Furness Railways who used her mainly for hiring out to private parties for only £350. Although* Britannia *was elegant it would be hard to find more perfect lines than the* Fairy Queen.

BAKED SALMON with CUCUMBER SAUCE

This was a favourite luncheon or supper dish in Victorian times. The salmon from the Solway is particularly fine. In the early years of the 19th century a lot of salmon came from Carlisle and West Cumberland and was sold for as little as 2d a pound. There was so much of it at one time, a rule was laid down that the boys of a charity school in Kendal were not to be 'compelled to dine on salmon or fish in general more than three days a week'.

1 salmon about 2.3 kg (5 lb)	a sprig of fresh fennel and parsley
a little oil or butter	salt and freshly ground white pepper

Few people today have a large fish kettle, but a simple yet excellent method is to use foil, especially if the fish is cut. (And when buying a piece, choose the tail end: it is both sweeter and has less bone.)

If the fish is to be eaten hot, then grease the foil well with melted butter, but if to be eaten cold use a little oil. If the fish is large, or long, then make two thick straps of foil and lay these over the sheet (to help to lift the fish after it is cooked). Then put the fish on top, tuck the herbs into the gullet and season well. Secure the foil over the top, twisting the cut edges well to make a loose, but firm parcel.

Then you can either stand it in a large baking dish and cook at 150°C (300°F) or gas mark 3 for 1 hour for a 2.3 kg (5 lb) salmon and for 10 minutes per 450 g (1 lb) for anything over. Or you can put it in a dish half full of cold water if you want the salmon hot, and let the water come to the boil; cook for up to 2.3 kg (5 lb) for 5 minutes per 450 g (1 lb), for fish up to 4.5 kg (10 lb) for about 50–60 minutes. Test to see if the fish comes away from the bone.

For hot fish, leave in the foil for 10 minutes, then open and remove the skin and side bones; for cold salmon leave it to cool in the foil, then skin.

CUCUMBER SAUCE

For serving with cold salmon. See that all ingredients are cold before starting. Peel and grate 1 small cucumber. Beat 300 ml (½ pint) cream until thick and add 1 teaspoon tarragon vinegar gradually and a good squeeze of lemon. Season to taste and just before serving mix in the grated cucumber.

Colonel G. J. M. Ridehalgh's steam yacht the Fairy Queen, *Windermere, c. 1860.*

ROAST, STUFFED HERDWICK LAMB or MUTTON with ONION SAUCE

'The afternoon was fine, and the road for full five miles runs along the side of Wyander-mere, with delicious views across it, and almost from one end to the other: it is ten miles in length and at most a mile over, resembling the course of some vast and magnificent river, but no flat marshy grounds, no osier beds, or patches of scrubby plantation on its banks: at the head two valleys open among the mountains ... in which Wrynose and Hard-knot, two great mountains rise above the rest.'   Thomas Gray 1716–71.

'Wynander-mere' became Windermere in the 19th century and has long been the scene of many regattas and races. See page 92. Celebrations were often held at the Ferry Inn, page 81, afterwards.

ROAST, STUFFED HERDWICK LAMB OR MUTTON WITH ONION SAUCE

1 boned leg of lamb or mutton
  about 2.3 kg (5 lb) in weight
2 tablespoons mutton dripping
  or oil
300 ml ($\frac{1}{2}$ pint) stock, red wine
  or cider

For the stuffing
3 rashers bacon, chopped
1 small onion
1 teaspoon chopped parsley
$\frac{1}{2}$ teaspoon chopped rosemary
4 rounded tablespoons
  breadcrumbs

For the sauce
3 large onions, peeled
2 tablespoons butter
1 level tablespoon flour
300 ml ($\frac{1}{2}$ pint) milk
$\frac{1}{4}$ teaspoon ground nutmeg
150 ml ($\frac{1}{4}$ pint) cream
salt and pepper

rind and juice of 1 lemon
salt and pepper

Mix all the stuffing ingredients together and put into the cavity left by the bone in the joint. Secure with small skewers and make any excess stuffing into small balls. Dust the skin with pepper and with a sharp knife score the skin with a diamond pattern. Put into the baking tin with the mutton dripping or about 3–4 tablespoons oil. Bake at 200°C (400°F) or gas mark 6 for half an hour and reduce to 180°C (350°F) or gas mark 4 for 20–25 minutes per 450 g (1 lb) depending on whether you like the meat well-cooked or not. Pour off any excess fat, put the meat on to a warmed serving dish and keep hot, then boil up the pan juices with the stock, wine or cider and seasoning until reduced.

To make the sauce, slice the onions thinly and soften them in the melted butter. Sprinkle the flour over, cook for 1 minute then add the milk and stir until it boils and is smooth and creamy. Add nutmeg and seasoning, then add the cream. Heat up but do not boil.

An alternative to serve with the meat is rowan jelly, page 20.

DAMSON PUNCH

Mix together 1 bottle damson wine, see page 20, and 600 ml (1 pint) boiling water and heat but do not boil. Add 125 ml ($\frac{1}{4}$ pint) rum, $\frac{1}{2}$ teaspoon ground nutmeg and a piece of stick cinnamon and blade mace. Sweeten to taste and pour over a sliced lemon in a large bowl. Serve hot on a cold day and over ice on a hot day. Enough for 16–18 drinks.

Hen Holme *at the finish, Windermere, 1880.*

BAKED LAKE TROUT

A regatta was held in honour of Queen Victoria's Golden Jubilee, and in the same year the Windermere Yacht Club became 'Royal' due to Sir William Forwood's connection with Queen Victoria's secretary, Ponsonby. Colonel Ridehalgh's steamer Britannia *can be seen moored in the photograph, see also page 89.*

There have been regattas on Windermere since early in the 19th century, and even before that there were races for rowing skiffs. The following is an account of the regatta on Windermere in 1818 when Sir Walter Scott together with his daughter and future son-in-law J. G. Lockhart visited Windermere to stay with friends.

'There were brilliant cavalcades through the woods in the mornings, and delicious boatings on the lake by moonlight, and the last day "The Admiral of the Lake" presided over one of the most splendid regattas that ever enlivened Windermere ... The Three Bards of the Lakes led the cheers that hailed Scott and Canning; and the music and sunshine, flags, streamers, and gay dresses, the merry hum of voices, and the rapid splashings of innumerable oars, made up a dazzling mixture of sensations, as the flotilla wound its way among richly-foliaged islands, and along bays and promontories peopled with enthusiastic spectators.'

From Life of Scott *by J. G. Lockhart.*

BAKED LAKE TROUT

4 lake trout weighing about 450 g (1 lb) each	4 sprigs each: fresh parsley and lemon thyme
75 g (3 oz) butter	150 m ($\frac{1}{4}$ pint) dry white wine
salt and freshly ground white pepper	1 large lemon

Clean the fish, wash and wipe dry. Then finely chop the herbs and mix them into 50 g (2 oz) butter. Divide this butter between the fish putting it into the gullet. Lay the fish head to tail closely in a fireproof dish and season to taste. Pour the wine over, cover with foil and cook in a moderate oven, 180°C (350°F) or gas mark 4, for about 20 minutes. Take out and add the remainder of the butter cut into small pieces, cover and continue cooking for a further 7 minutes. Garnish with 4 lemon wedges. Serves 4.

Note: if the trout are small, they are best stuffed with the herb butter as above, then rubbed all over with seasoning, the rest of the butter, and grilled on each side under a moderate grill for about 5 minutes on each side rather than baked.

POTTED TROUT

This is a very old recipe and it makes an excellent cold dish. Clean about 6 trout, wash them with a little wine vinegar, slit down the back and take out the backbone and rib bones. Salt and pepper them inside and put them head to tail in an ovenproof dish with about 1 tablespoon butter over each. Sprinkle with a pinch of mace, nutmeg and clove, cover, and bake in a slow oven, 150°C (300°F) or gas mark 2, for 1 hour. Remove from the liquid, put into a clean dish with a little of the liquor, and when cold cover all over with fresh melted butter. Serve cold.

Awaiting the prize-giving for the races of the regatta, in the grounds of the Ferry Inn Hotel, 25 July 1887.

FRIED PERCH

The beautiful lakes in this part of the world offer many varieties of boating. There are also many kinds of fish to be found, one such as the char (see page 96) being particular to Windermere.

'One summer evening (led by her) I found
A little boat tied to a willow tree
Within a rocky cave, its usual home.
Straight I unloosed her chain, and stepping in
Pushed from the shore ...'

From The Prelude, William Wordsworth, 1770–1850

FRIED PERCH

Perch (*Perca fluviatilis*) is one of the most delicate-tasting of all fresh-water fish and it is prolific in the Lakes. It is handsome to look at, olive-green on top, yellow below with bright red fins. The spines of the fins need careful handling as they can sting quite badly. It can attain a length of 35 cm (14 in) but more generally those caught are about 25 to 30 cm (10 to 12 in) in length. Large ones can be poached and served as for pike, page 124, but the smaller ones are delicious fried.

It is wise to wear rubber gloves for cleaning the fish because of the spines: head and gut the fish, cut off the fins, then slip a sharp knife under the skin just above the tail and quickly strip the skin off. If small leave whole, but for larger fish remove the backbone and small side bones. Wash and dry well.

Boating on the lake, c. 1870s.

For the batter

125 g (4 oz) flour	4 cleaned perch about 20 cm
1 separated egg	(8 in) long
salt and pepper	6 tablespoons oil
approximately 4 tablespoons	1 large lemon
beer or ale	4–6 sprigs parsley

Mix the flour with the egg yolk and the seasoning, and beat well until smooth. Then thin down with the beer, beating well. Leave to stand for about 20 minutes. Just before cooking beat the eggwhite until stiff and gently fold into the batter. It should be quite thick, and may not need the entire eggwhite if the egg was large. Dip the fish into this so that it is thoroughly coated all over. Heat up the oil and fry the fish on both sides turning once so that they are golden brown and crisp. In the same oil fry the whole sprigs of parsley and serve crisp around the fish with wedges of lemon.

This also makes a good breakfast dish and it is delicious served with rashers of crisp bacon.

POTTED CHAR

The char is a little known member of the salmon family, Salmo salvelinus, confined to very deep lakes, but most common in Windermere where it is a local delicacy. It has pinkish flesh not unlike a salmon trout, but its flavour is even more delicate. In the 17th, 18th and 19th centuries it was so popular that there was a danger of it being overfished, for char pie and potted char were used as 'instruments of social diplomacy'; potted char was put into extremely fine hand-painted ceramic pots which nowadays are collectors' items. Potted char was considered a fine breakfast dish with toast.

'Among the great variety of fish, which inhabit the extensive waters of this lake, the char is the most remarkable. It is near twice the size of a herring. Its back is of an olive-green: its belly of a light vermilion; softening in some parts into white: and changing into a deep red, at the insertion of the fins.

'A parcel of char, just caught, and thrown together into the luggage-pool of a boat makes a pleasant harmony of colour. The green olive-tint prevails; to which a spirit is here and there given a light blush of vermilion ... These pleasing colours are assisted by the bright silvery lights, which play over the whole; and which nothing reflects more beautifully than the scales of the fish.'
Char Fishing in Windermere, *William Gilpin, 1724–1804.*

'I received yours of the 1st. this month, and also the Pott of Charr which you sent by that day's Carrier, which was the best I ever eat, and I would have you send me some of the same sort every Carryer, take care to pick the hen fish and those that are of the Red Kind, and let them be potted and seasoned just as that Pot was, for it cant be better.' A letter sent from the Duke of Montagu to Mr Atkinson of Dalton, 27 January 1738.

POTTED CHAR

'Cut off the fins and cheek part of each side of the head of your chars, rip them open, take out the guts, and the blood from the backbone, dry them well in a cloth, lay them on a board and throw on them a good deal of salt. Let them stand all night, then scrape it gently off them and wipe them exceedingly well with a cloth. Pound some mace, cloves and nutmeg very fine, throw a little inside of them and a good deal of salt and pepper on the outside. Put them close down in a deep pot with their bellies up with plenty of clarified butter over them. Set them in the oven and let them stand for three hours. [Oven should be at the lowest.] When they come out pour what butter you can off clear, lay a board over them and turn them upside down to let the gravy run from them. Scrape the salt and pepper very carefully off and season them exceedingly well both inside and out with the above seasoning, lay them close in broad thin pots for that purpose, with their backs up. Then cover them well with clarified butter. Keep them in a cool dry place.' From *The Experienced English Housekeeper*, by Mrs Elizabeth Raffald, 1769.

Char can also be cooked or potted as for trout, page 92.

Fishing for char, Windermere, c. 1890s.

COCKLES

COCKLES

There are over two hundred varieties of cockles which are members of the *Cardium* family, and first cousins of the clam. They are small bivalves with radial shell markings, and it is quite difficult to distinguish them from their better known cousins. However they have a smooth surface with a slight ridge running vertically over the shell.

Cockles are still popular in the Lake District and served in many ways. The curious wooden contraption in the photograph is used to bang on the sands, this shocks the cockles into burrowing down squirting a jet of water as they do so, which betrays their position.

They are good used in a shellfish soup, either on their own or with a mixture of shellfish such as scallops, mussels and periwinkles.

COCKLE SOUP

40 cockles	2 tablespoons each: finely
2 heaped tablespoons butter	chopped onion and celery
2 heaped tablespoons flour	2 tablespoons chopped parsley
900 ml (1½ pints) cockle liquor	salt and pepper
600 ml (1 pint) creamy milk	a little cream to garnish

Scrub the cockles well to get rid of the grit and sand. Then put them into a large saucepan with sea-water (or well salted water) to cover. Bring gently to the boil shaking the pan from time to time and as soon as the shells open they are ready. Do not continue cooking as this toughens them. When cool take them from the shells. Strain the

Cockling at low tide, Morecambe Bay, c. 1920.

liquor and put aside. Make up to the required amount if necessary.

Melt the butter in a saucepan, stir in the flour and let it cook for 1 minute. Add the cockle liquor and milk, stirring all the time to avoid lumps. When smooth add the onion and celery and cook for about 5 to 7 minutes or until soft. Add the parsley and season to taste. Finally add the cockles, heat and serve with a spoonful of cream in each bowl. Serves about 6.

BOILED COCKLES

These are often eaten cooked as in the first stage above and served with a squeeze of lemon juice or vinegar. If served hot they are good with melted butter as well.

COCKLES AND TATIE-POT

Recently in Whitehaven I was served with a tatie-pot (see page 35) which had been cooked with a layer of cockles on the top. It was excellent and not unlike the taste that oysters can give to a steak and kidney pudding.

MORECAMBE BAY SHRIMPS

Morecambe Bay and the villages around have long been famous for the tiny shrimps (*Crangon crangon*) which do not ever get larger than a little over 2.5 cm (1 in) long. The edible part is even smaller and shelling them is a tiresome business. It is still done by hand at Flookburgh, the nimble fingers of the fish-sellers deftly shelling rapidly while talking to you. But they are delicious to eat once the labour is done. When raw they are greyish and almost transparent, but cooked they become pink. I think that steaming is the best way for them, no flavour is lost in these delicate morsels. Steam over boiling water for no longer than 5 minutes, then cool before shelling.

Once shelled they can be used in many ways: as they are served on a bed of lettuce and perhaps a squeeze of lemon; in a cocktail, but beware you do not make the dressing too strong. Home-made mayonnaise with lemon and a dash of tabasco is enough. In pancakes they are delicious, also in omelettes and they are perfect for a sauce to serve with a larger fish such as plaice, sole, haddock, etc. Allow 125 g (4 oz) shelled shrimps for every 300 ml (½ pint) white sauce made from half fish stock and half milk.

POTTED SHRIMPS

This method is the traditional way and is famous all over England as a first course with thin toast, or brown bread and butter.

450 g (1 lb) picked Morecambe Bay shrimps

175 g (6 oz) unsalted butter

salt, cayenne pepper and nutmeg to flavour

Heat all but 25 g (1 oz) of the butter but do not let it oil. Then add the shrimps and stir until they are coated. Season to taste and mix well. Pour into small dishes and leave to set. Then heat up the remaining butter and pour over the top of each dish to seal the contents. This way they will keep in a cold place for several days. Use the top butter to spread on the toast when serving. Serves 4.

FLUKES

These are a fish used locally: a flat fish with longish tails often found in the fishermen's nets which mark the sides in a diamond pattern. Flukes are a firm, white fish with a good flavour and should be tried. They are Witch Flounder (*Glyptocephalus cynoglossus*) and when found in the deep North Atlantic reach a length of about 90 cm (3 ft). However these seldom attain more than 30 cm (1 ft) at the most. They are good cleaned, gutted and either baked with a little butter or seasoned and fried in butter, then served with fresh melted butter which has a good squeeze of lemon in it.

Paddling on the east coast, c. 1905.

FRIED GUDGEON

It is possible that the boys opposite were fishing for gudgeon (Gobio gobio) *a small freshwater fish of the carp family found on the sandy bottom of most rivers and lakes of Europe. The river looks too small at this point for them to have been 'tickling' trout.*

'They fished in the Brathay river, just where it enters the Lake, and there found some most peculiar fish which they had never seen before . . . lo and behold! there were, after more than fifty years, the offspring of his own gudgeon.'
From A Servant of the Empire *by Clara Boyle, c. 1920s.*

FRIED GUDGEON

Gudgeon is a small fish often used as a garnish for larger fish: it is delicious for breakfast, gutted, dipped in a batter, see page 95, and fried for breakfast with crisp rashers of bacon.

If small, clean them, cut off the heads and tails and roll them in seasoned flour. Heat up about 4–6 tablespoons oil and when it is hot but not smoking fry the fish on both sides, then drain on kitchen paper. Serve with salt and lemon.

SAUCER PANCAKES

This is an old Westmorland recipe kindly given to me by Mrs Johnson of Tullythwaite House, Underbarrow, near Kendal, who serves fine dinners and teas at her 17th-century farmhouse.

50 g (2 oz) butter   2 eggs, beaten

50 g (2 oz) sugar   300 ml (½ pint) milk
50 g (2 oz) flour

First lightly butter 4 ovenproof saucers. Then beat butter and sugar to a cream and add the beaten eggs alternately with the flour. Gradually add the milk and beat until it is a smooth paste.

Divide between the 4 saucers and leave to stand for half an hour. Bake in a moderate oven, 180°C (350°F) or gas mark 4, for 10–15 minutes until firm. Turn out on to sugared paper, spread with jam and fold over.

DAMSON JAM

Made from the good damsons of the Lyth Valley, and very popular.

1.4 kg (3 lb) damsons   450 ml (¾ pint) water
1.4 kg (3 lb) sugar   juice of 1 lemon

Either stone the damsons first or cook them and then stone them. They should be cooked, just brought to the boil and then simmered for 30 minutes or until tender. Add the sugar and also the lemon juice, and bring slowly to the boil, stirring all the time to make certain the sugar has dissolved. Then boil rapidly for about 12–15 minutes until setting point is reached.

Pour into warm, sterilized jars filled to the top, cover, tie down and keep in a cool place. Makes about 2.7 kg (6 lb) jam.

Boys grappling for fish, c. 1890s.

LAKE TROUT

Wastwater is an isolated lake west of the Derwent surrounded by mountains, the Screes, with a magnificent view of Great Gable. It has been described as a wonder lake, the surface 60 m (200 ft) above the sea, and about a third of the floor goes below sea-level. The average depth is 40 m (135 ft), much greater than that of any of the other lakes, and it is but rarely frozen, possibly because the surface always seems to be ruffling in the breeze. From here to Wasdale Head is considered one of the most wild and beautiful in the Lake District with firs and larches, bracken, heather and ling. The rich red and brown tints of the rocks on Wastwater Scree are due to a surface vein of ironstone so pure and soft that for many years it was regularly collected by shepherds and used as 'ruddle' to mark their sheep, for not only was the colour strong but impervious to moisture and would remain until next shearing-time.

It is famous for the numbers of illustrious people who have climbed these mountains, but the angling in Wastwater is also very good and excellent fishing can be found there.

'Is this the Lake, the cradle of the storms,
Where silence never tames the mountain-roar,
Where poets fear their self-created forms,
Or, sunk in trance severe, their God adore?
Is this the Lake, for ever dark and loud
With wave and tempest, cataract and cloud?'

Christopher North (Professor Wilson)
editor of Blackwood's Magazine, *1785–1854.*

LAKE TROUT

Freshly caught lake trout are a true delicacy and the sooner they are eaten the better they will be. For a special occasion have them for breakfast prepared as follows: Take 4 medium-sized fresh trout, clean them but leave the heads on, and roll them in seasoned flour. Fry about 8 rashers of good, sweet bacon and when it is crisp put it on a warmed dish and keep warm. Quickly fry the trout in the bacon fat on both sides, and do not salt them until they are cooked and you have tasted them, although a little pepper will not come amiss. Serve at once with crisp, hot toast and farm butter and you have a meal for the Gods.

Note: if the trout are large you can fillet them first by cutting them with a sharp knife along the spine bone, but the bone does act as an inner baste and they are quite easy to dissect. If a nutty taste is liked then roll the fish in fine oatmeal instead of the flour, or use wholemeal flour instead of white.

Climbing gear in the entrance hall of Wastwater House Hotel, Easter 1895.

KENDAL MINT CAKE

KENDAL MINT CAKE

'We had attained the object of this journey; but our ambition now mounted higher. We saw the summit of Scafell, apparently very near to us; and we shaped our course towards it ... But discovering that it could not be reached without first making a considerable descent, we resolved, instead, to aim at another point of the same mountain, called the Pike, which I have since found has been estimated as higher than the summit bearing the name of Scafell Head ... The sun had never once been overshadowed by a cloud during the whole of our progress from the centre of Borrowdale. On the summit ... which we gained after much toil ... there was not a breath of air to stir even the papers containing our refreshments as they lay spread on a rock ... I ought to have mentioned that round the top of Scafell Pike not a blade of grass is to be seen. Cushions or tufts of moss, parched and brown, appear between the huge blocks and stones that lie in heaps on all sides to a great distance, like skeletons or bones of the earth not needed at the creation, and there left to be covered with never-dying lichens, which the clouds and dews nourish, and adorned with colours of vivid and exquisite beauty.

'... the great hub of the wheel of mountains'.

William Wordsworth.

Scafell is 963 m (3,210 ft) high and that part above the 900 m (3,000 ft) contour was dedicated to the nation by Lord Leconfield as a tribute to the heroism of the men from the dales who fought in World War I. Scafell still attracts serious climbers from all over.

Kendal Mint Cake is made in Kendal by several different manufacturers. It is not a cake but a delicious candy-like sweetmeat, firm and minty, ideal for nibbling under strenuous climbing conditions. Romney's (George Romney, the famous painter was born in Kendal in 1734) mint cake has been taken on many mountaineering expeditions and was amongst the provisions carried by Sir Edmund Hillary and Sirdar Tensing when climbing Mount Everest. When they reached the summit on 29 May 1953, he wrote: 'We sat on the snow and looked at the country far below us ... we nibbled Kendal Mint Cake.' Another member of the expedition wrote: 'It was easily the most popular item on our high altitude ration – our only criticism was that we did not have enough of it.'

It is commercially made in three varieties: white, brown and chocolate covered.

400 g (14 oz) sugar (use soft brown sugar for the brown kind)	1 teaspoon peppermint essence
	150 ml ($\frac{1}{4}$ pint) milk or mixed milk and water
50 g (2 oz) glucose powder	

Boil the sugar, glucose and milk to 116°C (240°F), the 'soft ball' stage. Take from the heat and add the peppermint, then beat thoroughly until it is smooth and about to set. Pour into an oiled tin to a depth of 0.3–0.5 cm ($\frac{1}{8}$–$\frac{1}{4}$ in) and mark into large squares just before it sets.

'Gaston' and George Abraham the photographer, climbing Scafell Pinnacle, c. 1890s.

WINDERMERE SPICE BISCUITS

The Lakes have been the scenes of many 'firsts' in the field of modern inventions: Coniston is the lake where record water speeds were attained first by Sir Malcolm Campbell and later by his son Donald, and Windermere has seen many innovations. The Water Hen was a land plane fitted with floats and it was owned by Captain Edward Wakefield a Kendal manufacturer. On 30 April 1912, it made its first flight from Hill of Oaks, near the southern end of Windermere, piloted by Mr Stanley Adams. There was no chassis or protection from the weather and the front bamboo elevator rod, ten foot long, came directly to the joystick. The rotary engine, a five-cylinder Gnome, spun around a stationary crankshaft. It was lubricated by castor oil and had a pusher propeller. It was a two-seater and passengers paid a minimum of £2 per trip. It was a most successful waterplane and went on until late into 1916. Naturally some people were wary of this new and strange-looking machine and the writer Beatrix Potter showed alarm lest it should frighten horses on the ferry.

There was also another pioneer flyer called Oscar Gnosspelius who after several failures was successful with his monoplane to which he fitted floats in February 1912. Frank Herbert the young Bowness man who came from a family of photographers, his father had started a studio there in the 1880s, took the first aerial view of Bowness from the Water Hen as it flew over Windermere at a speed of forty-five miles an hour.

WINDERMERE SPICE BISCUITS

These could have been pleasant to nibble while flying over the lake on a cold day.

125 g (4 oz) butter or margarine	1 level teaspoon caraway seeds
125 g (4 oz) brown sugar	1 level teaspoon ground
175 g (6 oz) self raising flour	cinnamon
	1 large egg, well beaten

Cream the butter and sugar, then by hand add the sifted flour, the caraway seeds and the cinnamon alternately with the well beaten egg. Work it quickly and roll into a ball. Turn out on to a lightly floured surface and roll out to about 1.5 cm ($\frac{1}{2}$ in) thick. Cut into small rounds with a pastry cutter and put on to a lightly greased baking sheet, well spaced. Bake at 180°C (350°F) or gas mark 4 for about 20 minutes. Cool on a wire rack. Makes about 20 small biscuits.

The Water Hen *flying over Windermere after take-off, c. 1912.*

PHEASANT WITH CELERY AND CREAM

Originally the Old England Hotel was a private house owned by a Captain Elms. During that time it was said to be haunted by the ghost of a man who had been murdered by his butler. The butler had escaped, but the ghost of the victim and immovable stains of blood were said to be found in the dining room. However after a lot of rebuilding it became an hotel in the 1880s and neither ghost nor bloodstains were ever seen again.

It is still a fine hotel today and the front looks very similar to the photograph.

PHEASANT WITH CELERY AND CREAM

There is quite a lot of game for such a small region in the Lake District, and certain areas are noted for the different kinds: ducks from Derwentwater, see page 19, hares from Greystoke, pigeons from Crosthwaite and pheasants from Underbarrow.

This is an excellent way of serving pheasant which is not perhaps in its first youth, the bird is always beautifully moist. It is also very good for a plump capon or chicken.

1 large well-hung pheasant	150 ml ($\frac{1}{4}$ pint) port
75 g (3 oz) butter	2 hearts of celery, cut into
2 rashers bacon, diced	rounds and blanched
a little flour	1 beaten eggyolk
300 ml ($\frac{1}{2}$ pint) chicken stock	300 ml ($\frac{1}{2}$ pint) cream
1 heaped teaspoon chopped parsley	salt and pepper

Heat the butter in an ovenproof dish and brown the bird all over. Add the chopped bacon and let it brown a little, then take off any excess fat. Sprinkle a little flour over and turn the bird. Add the stock, herbs and port and season to taste. Cover and cook in the oven at 180°C (350°F) or gas mark 4 for about $\frac{1}{2}$ hour. Then add the celery which has been cut into rounds and blanched. Cover again and continue cooking for about 35 minutes or until the bird is tender.

Remove from the oven, lift out the bird and the celery on to a warmed serving dish and keep warm. Mix the eggyolk with the cream and very gradually stir it into the hot stock of the bird. Heat up, but do not reboil for fear of curdling. Serve separately in a sauce boat. The bird can be carved before taking it to table and some of the sauce poured over; the rest should be put into a sauce boat. Serves 4.

Four-in-hand coach outside the Old England Hotel, Bowness, on Windermere, c. 1880s.

ROAST VENISON

The drive across the Honister Pass is said to be one of the most spectacular in England, but it was notoriously hard on the horses. It was formerly the route taken by the slate quarrymen and the scree on the roads makes walking hazardous. The top of the pass is (1,190 ft) above sea level, and nowadays it is easily negotiable by car.

ROAST VENISON

The Lake District has many forests which contain red, roe and fallow deer; from time to time these are culled to keep down numbers and to ensure healthy herds. It is advisable to marinade venison before cooking and this marinade is also good for hare, wood pigeon or other elderly game birds. It can also be casseroled as beef, page 43.

For the marinade

1 bottle red wine	1 sliced onion or 2 shallots
150 ml (¼ pint) olive oil	6 allspice berries
1 sprig rosemary	10 black peppercorns, whole
1 bay leaf	

For the roast

1 haunch or shoulder venison about 2.3 kg (5 lb)	1 teaspoon brown sugar squeeze of lemon
4 rashers bacon	salt and pepper
½ teaspoon each: ground ginger, cinnamon	2 tablespoons rowan or redcurrant jelly (page 20)

Mix all the marinade ingredients together and put the meat into it; cover and leave for about 2 days, turning several times each day so that all the joint is immersed. To cook, take the joint out, pat it dry, then rub it with the brown sugar, ginger and cinnamon mixed together and wrap the bacon rashers over the top. Put into a roasting pan and pour around about half of the strained marinade which has been gently boiled. Cover with a piece of foil or greaseproof paper and roast in a moderate to hot oven, 200°C (400°F) or gas mark 6, for 30 minutes, then reduce the heat to 180°C (350°F) or gas mark 4 and continue cooking for 30 minutes per 450 g (1 lb), basting every half hour. When ready, remove to a warmed dish and keep hot. Scrape down the side of the pan, add the rest of the marinade, season, then add the lemon juice and the rowan jelly. Stir well, boil up to reduce by about half and serve separately. Enough for 10–12 people. Hot red cabbage is traditionally eaten with game.

HOT RED CABBAGE

Shred a medium-sized red cabbage, and put into a saucepan with about 2 cooking apples chopped, peeled and cored, 2 teaspoons brown sugar, 3 cloves, 1 medium finely chopped onion, 600 ml (1 pint) stock or water, salt and pepper and about 3 tablespoons red wine (or use some marinade) or wine vinegar. Bring to the boil, then simmer gently, turning from time to time for about 2–3 hours. It actually improves with long slow cooking, and can be reheated too.

Four-in-hands descending Honister Pass, c. 1890. Photographed by G. Abraham.

CUMBERLAND CAKE

Castlerigg Stone Circle is often called the 'Druids' Circle' which is quite inaccurate. It dates in fact from about 1800 to 1500 BC and was built by people of the Bronze Age who came from France and Spain. Castlerigg has a kind of internal chamber but it is not certain that this was part of the original construction. It is however positioned on the most magnificent site and surrounded by mountains, the furthest away being the Helvellyn range. Access to it is easily made from the road, across a field.

'Bade farewell to Keswick and took the Ambleside road in a gloomy morning; wind east and afterwards north east; about two miles from the town mounted an eminence called Castle Rigg, and the sun breaking out discovered the most beautiful view I have yet seen of the whole valley behind me, the two lakes, the river, the mountain, all in their glory! had almost a mind to have gone back again.' Thomas Gray, 1716–1771.

CUMBERLAND CAKE

This is a traditional cake which is what we could call a tart or pie nowadays.

275 g (10 oz) shortcrust pastry (see page 87)	1 heaped tablespoon butter
75 g (3 oz) brown sugar	1 eggwhite, stiffly beaten with 1 tablespoon castor sugar
225 g (8 oz) mixed currants, raisins, sultanas and chopped peel	2 tablespoons rum or squeeze of lemon, optional

First make the pastry and let it rest in a cold place for at least half an hour. Then lightly grease a 20 cm (8 in) pie plate and roll out half the pastry to fit it. Prick the bottom with a fork. Mix together the sugar, butter and the mixed fruit and peel. Put this over the pastry, and if using the rum or lemon juice add that too. Roll out the remaining pastry and cover the top, dampening the edges well so that they are secure. Then notch them with a fork or the finger and thumb.

Bake at 200°C (400°F) or gas mark 6 for about 25–30 minutes or until the pastry is a pale gold. Then spread over the top with the beaten eggwhite which has been sweetened with a little sugar. Put back in the oven to set and to brown slightly.

It is very good cut into wedges and served warm. Serves 6–8.

Castlerigg Stone Circle, near Keswick, c. 1880.

WHITE MOSS CUMBERLAND NICKY

The village band photographed has a variety of instruments, and the three-horse bus regularly met trains at Windermere station. Edgar's drapers had formerly been Atkinson's stationers and drapers combined.

The Royal Hotel in the background was originally called after its famous hotelier-owner, John Ullock, although officially its name was the White Lion. However, after a visit in 1840 by the dowager Queen Adelaide who stayed for a weekend, it was called the 'Royal'. It was a weekend of festivity for the villagers and on the Saturday tables were laid in the street 'to regail the poor inhabitants of Bowness and neighbourhood with tea'. Even rain did not dampen the spirits; after removing to a nearby schoolhouse, there was dancing which went on into the early hours of the morning in the street in front of the hotel.

WHITE MOSS CUMBERLAND NICKY

Recipe kindly given by Mrs Jean Butterworth of the White Moss Hotel, Rydal Water, Grasmere.

225 g (8 oz) rich shortcrust pastry (see page 87)	1 heaped tablespoon Demerara sugar
125 g (4 oz) dates	2 tablespoons rum
1 tablespoon water	50 g (2 oz) butter
3 medium cooking apples	a little milk

Chop and stone the dates and add the water. Soften them over a low heat, then cool. Roll out the pastry, cut into half and line a 17–20 cm (7–8 in) pie plate with it. Put in the peeled, cored and sliced apples and scatter with the sugar. Mix the rum with the butter into the dates and spread over the apples, then top with a pastry lid. Lightly prick the top, brush with milk and bake at 200°C (400°F) or gas mark 6 for 15 minutes, then lower the heat to 180°C (350°F) or gas mark 4 for a further 15 minutes, or until the top is golden brown. Serve cut into wedges, hot or cold, with cream.

There are several traditional recipes for 'nickies': a very old one omits the dates and apples but uses 75 g (3 oz) currants flavoured with $\frac{1}{2}$ teaspoon grated nutmeg.

SATURDAY SPECIAL PUDDING

This is an old recipe traditionally used at Outgate. Cream together 225 g (4 oz) each of butter and sugar: then beat in 2 eggs. Mix together 225 g (4 oz) plain flour, $\frac{1}{2}$ teaspoon baking powder and stir into this mixture, and finally add 50 g (2 oz) grated coconut soaked in about 3 tablespoons of milk. Pour into a lightly buttered pie dish and bake at 170°C (325°F) or gas mark 3 for about 1 hour. Serve hot with cream or fresh home-made custard. Serves 4.

Bowness on Windermere en fête *for Queen Victoria's Diamond Jubilee in 1897.*

HIRING-FAIR CAKES

Moot Hall, Keswick, was first used as a courthouse and prison. It was rebuilt in 1571 by the intercession of Richard Dudley of Yanworth and was used to house the copper ingots made at the works at Brigham by the Greta River. The present Moot Hall was begun in 1695, the first lease being granted by Sir Francis Radcliffe. It was rebuilt in 1813. Keswick is an extensive town which was once well known for mining both copper and graphite (see page 62) and for markets and fairs. There was a hiring fair held there up until the early years of this century where servants and farm labourers gathered to be hired, which although grim, was made into a festival for the workers with many entertainments, sideshows and beer drinking.

In 1875 the first interdenominational religious convention was held there in the third week in July, originally for two weeks, but nowadays it lasts only for a week. In the past Keswick had great literary associations (see page 19), and in later years the writer Sir Hugh Walpole settled on the Portinscale side of Derwentwater.

'We got in in the evening, travelling in a post-chaise from Penrith, in the midst of a gorgeous sunshine which transmuted all the mountains into colours ... We thought we had come into fairyland!'   Charles Lamb's Letters, 1802.

HIRING-FAIR CAKES

These cakes used to be made at Whitsun and Martinmas for the Hiring Fair.

125 g (4 oz) each: butter or margarine and lard	2 teaspoons white sugar
	12 g (½ oz) fresh yeast

450 g (1 lb) plain flour	120 ml (scant ¼ pint) warm water
½ teaspoon salt	

Rub the fats into the mixed dry ingredients and make a well in the centre. Mix the yeast with the tepid water, leave to work in a warm place for 10 minutes, and pour into the well. Sprinkle the flour over, cover and leave for about 40 minutes. Then punch down and knead a little, turn out on to a lightly floured surface and roll out very thinly. Cut into 10 cm (4 in) squares about 12 of them, but see that you have an even number.

For the filling

450 g (1 lb) currants	a pinch of nutmeg or mace
225 g (8 oz) soft brown sugar	½ teaspoon ground allspice
50 g (2 oz) finely chopped mixed peel	2–3 teaspoons rum and 2 tablespoons cold tea

Mix all the ingredients together and let them soak for about half an hour. Then put a tablespoon of this mixture on half of each of the above squares, dampen the edges cover with the remainder of the squares, pressing and pinching down the edges so that the filling is secured. Bake at 210°C (425°F) or gas mark 7 for about 25–30 minutes or until the squares are golden brown.

Main Street, Keswick, with Moot Hall in centre, 1888.

CUMBERLAND SAUSAGE PIE

The coming of the railway to Windermere from Kendal in 1847 made an enormous difference to the life of the people, for Windermere had been a small hamlet with perhaps six or so houses. However, Bowness was a flourishing village at that time with shops, the famous St Martin's church with its stained glass dating from 1300 (the building itself dates from 1443), several inns and two or three hotels. There is still a Chestnut Tree Café in Bowness Main Street, although the frontage and décor have changed vastly.

CUMBERLAND SAUSAGE PIE

This is excellent when made with Cumberland sausage (see page 32) but it is still a good dish when made with sausagemeat. It makes splendid picnic fare.

For the flaky pastry
450 g (1 lb) plain flour
pinch of salt
squeeze of lemon juice
450 g (1 lb) butter or firm
  margarine
3 tablespoons iced water
a little milk for wash

For the filling
450 g (1 lb) Cumberland sausage
  or sausagemeat
2 rashers bacon, rinded and diced
pinch each: dried sage and lemon
  thyme
1 tablespoon chopped parsley
pepper and pinch of nutmeg
4 eggs

First make the pastry by sieving the flour into a bowl with the salt, then add the squeeze of lemon juice. Rub 2 tablespoons butter into the flour and add just enough iced water to make a firm dough. Turn out on to a floured board and roll to a rectangle about 1.5 cm ($\frac{1}{2}$ in) thick. Put the whole of the remaining butter which should be soft, in the middle, fold over, press the edges well and leave to stand for 15 minutes. With the sealed edges away from you roll out the pastry until it is 3 times the size. Then fold into 3, envelope style, turn the open edge to face you and roll again. Leave to rest as before, repeat the folding, rolling and resting, so that in all the pastry has been rolled and rested 6 times. If it still looks fat-streaked give it an extra roll. Wrap in greaseproof paper and chill for at least 1 hour. Or it can be frozen for future use.

To use roll out two-thirds of the pastry on a lightly floured surface and line a 18 cm (7 in) flan ring. Do not trim away any surplus. Skin the sausage. Derind and dice the bacon and mix it with the sausagemeat, herbs and some pepper. Brown it in a hot pan, but it is not necessary to cook it through. Spread it over the pastry, sprinkle with a little ground nutmeg, then make 4 indentations in the meat. Break an egg into each hollow and season them. Cover the top with the remaining pastry, folding the rim over the lid and dampening the edges a little so that it is secure. Press down the edges and trim with a sharp knife. Make a small slit on the top, then brush with the milk and bake at 220°C (425°F) or gas mark 7 for 15 minutes. Reduce to 170°C (325°F) or gas mark 3 for a further 15 minutes, or until it is golden. Serve hot or cold.

The railway parcel delivery cart opposite the Chestnut Tree Café, Bowness on Windermere, c. 1890.

WESTMORLAND STEAK

The view from Great Gable mountain is superb, and it is a favourite of climbers. It can be climbed either from Sty Head, or from Sty Head Tarn by Aaron Slack and Wind Gap which lies on the northeastern side of the mountain between Great and Green Gables. Great Gable has three great climbing grounds: the Napes Ridges and Kern Knotts to the south and the northern precipices. The summit crags above the Napes are called the Westmorland Crags, and they look down into the dense, dark ravine of Piers Ghyll.

Great Gable is 885 m (2,949 ft) high and on a boulder near the summit cairn is the war memorial tablet of the Fell and Rock Climbing Club to their members who fell during World War I. It is made of bronze and on it is engraved a relief map of the neighbouring peaks, those purchased by the club and presented to the nation through the National Trust being enclosed by a delimiting line.

WESTMORLAND STEAK

There was not a great deal of beef eaten by Cumbrian folk as sheep are the chief industry, but a quantity of beef was cured at Martinmas, the greatest part of which they pickled in brine, and the rest was dried and smoked. Every family in the 18th and early 19th century boiled a piece of salt meat on Sunday morning and ate it hot with an oatmeal pudding, then cold with oat bread or cakes, and soup was made from the stock.

900 g (2 lb) stewing steak, 4 cm (1½ in) thick	a little flour
	salt and pepper
1 tablespoon parsley	25 g (1 oz) butter or
1 medium onion	3 tablespoons oil
2 bay leaves	600 ml (1 pint) beef stock

Trim the steak and score it diamond fashion with a sharp knife. Finely chop the parsley and onion and rub this into the cuts all over. Cover and leave for about 1 hour to marinate. Then heat up the butter and dust the steak with pepper. When the butter is hot quickly fry the bay leaves, then the meat on both sides, salt it, and sprinkle with flour. Let the flour brown slightly, then add the beef stock and bring to the boil.

Put everything into an ovenproof dish, cover and cook in a slow to moderate oven, 170–180°C (325–350°F) or gas mark 3–4, for about 2 hours. Check once that the liquid is not drying up, if so add a little more stock. Serves 4.

Variation: the meat can be cut into largish cubes instead of leaving it in one piece and it is good with a cheese crust made as follows.

CHEESE PASTRY

Sift 125 g (4–5 oz) plain flour with a pinch of salt, and rub in 50 g (2 oz) fat, then add 75 g (3 oz) grated Cheddar cheese. Sprinkle this over the top and cook for 30 minutes.

Farmer driving his cattle with Great Gable in the background, c. 1900.

POACHED PIKE

There are many pike in the lakes and fishing for them has been traditional for centuries unlike many other parts of England where they are not often fished and used for food. Young pike, or pickerel weighing not more than about 4.5 kg (10 lb), are considered the best for eating and they can be cooked in many ways. Izaak Walton writing in 1653 says that 'it is a dish of meat too good for any but anglers, or very honest men.'

When William and Dorothy Wordsworth lived at Dove Cottage, Grasmere, William often fished for pike. In Dorothy's Journal for 11 June 1800 she writes: 'Wm and John went to the pike floats – they brought in 2 pikes'; and on the following day she records: 'We returned to dinner, 2 pikes boiled and roasted.' And yet another pike was caught on the following day.

POACHED PIKE

Two things should be noted about the pike, first that the scales should be removed by pouring boiling water over the fish until they dull, then it should be put into cold water and the scales scraped off with the back of a knife. Secondly to make the flesh more tender a handful of salt should be forced down the throat after catching and it should be left to hang overnight. This also makes the smaller bones disappear during cooking.

1 pike about 3 kg (7 lb)	1 tablespoon grated horseradish
1 bottle dry white wine	1 lemon
1 bay leaf	6 black peppercorns
a sprig thyme and parsley	1 blade mace
1 medium sliced onion	225 g (8 oz) unsalted butter

Clean the fish well and see that the scales are removed. Then put into a fish kettle with all the other ingredients except half the lemon and the butter. Fill with water, bring to the boil, then simmer gently for about 6 minutes per 450 g (1 lb) but test after half an hour that the flesh leaves the backbone easily. Lift out carefully on to a dish, remove the skin and serve with hot melted butter with a squeeze of lemon added.

If you don't have a pan large enough to take the fish, then either cut in half and wrap in cheesecloth and proceed as above; or wrap the whole fish in foil, secure well, put into a large baking tin and poach it in liquid in the oven for the same length of time.

It can also be served cold, garnished with stuffed hard-boiled eggs, tomatoes, olives and a Russian salad with a large bowl of home-made mayonnaise. Or if preferred some of the stock can be set with gelatine – 1 tablespoon to 600 ml (1 pint) of fish stock.

Young angler with a fine catch of pike, c. 1890s. Photographed by the Walmsley brothers.

INDEX